SUNY SERIES, PRAXIS: THEORY IN ACTION

Nancy A. Naples, editor

BTL

STATE UNIVERSITY OF NEW YORK PRESS *and* BETWEEN THE LINES

¡VIVA!

Community Arts and
Popular Education in the Americas

Deborah Barndt, editor
With VIVA! Project Partners

Dedicated to Raúl Leis (1947-2011)
VIVA partner and editor
Renowned writer, social movement leader
and popular educator of the Americas

Viva Raúl Leis, Viva!

Published by
STATE UNIVERSITY OF NEW YORK PRESS, ALBANY

© 2011 State University of New York

For information, contact State University of New York Press, Albany, NY
www.sunypress.edu

Production and book design, Laurie Searl
Marketing, Anne M. Valentine

Library of Congress Cataloging-in-Publication Data

¡VIVA! : community arts and popular education in the Americas / edited by
Deborah Barndt ; with VIVA! Project Partners.
     p. cm. — (SUNY series, Praxis : theory in action)
Includes bibliographical references and index.
   ISBN 978-1-4384-3766-8 (pbk. : alk. paper)
   ISBN 978-1-4384-3767-5 (hardcover : alk. paper)
 1. Community arts projects—Western Hemisphere. 2. Arts in education—
Western Hemisphere. I. Barndt, Deborah. II. Title: Community arts and popular
education in the Americas.
   NX180.A77V58 2011
   700.1'03097—dc22

                                    2011003194

Published in Canada by
BETWEEN THE LINES

401 Richmond Street West, Studio 277, Toronto, Ontario M5V 3A8, Canada
1-800-718-7201
www.btlbooks.com

Library and Archives Canada Cataloguing in Publication

¡VIVA! : community arts and popular education in the Americas / Deborah
Barndt, editor.
Accompanied by DVD.
Includes bibliographical references and index.
ISBN 978-1-926662-51-0 (pbk. : alk. paper)
1. Community arts projects—America.
2. Arts in education—America. I. Barndt, Deborah
NX180.A77V59 2011   700.1'03097   C2011-902938-3

Between the Lines gratefully acknowledges assistance for its publishing activities
from the Canada Council for the Arts, the Ontario Arts Council, the Government
of Ontario through the Ontario Book Publishers Tax Credit program and through
the Ontario Book Initiative, and the Government of Canada through the Canada
Book Fund.

Contents

Who, Why, and How VIVA?

> After listening to the stories of the VIVA projects, I hope you will say to yourself: "I am not alone." There is a very strong bond, a collective consciousness; there's someone who thinks like I do in Canada, in Panama, so I am not alone.
>
> —VIVA! Partner Sergio Eduardo (Lalo) Martínez Mayoral,
> Guadalajara, Mexico

This book has been created by and for people who are seeking a more just and sustainable world, who want to integrate education and art into community work, who believe that such synergy can foster greater passion for and deeper commitment to movements for social and environmental justice. It offers stories and experiences from the Global North and Global South that both support and challenge this work, that help build a bond between us as we work in our different communities to unveil and transform power. Hopefully it will make you, the reader—whether you are a student, educator, artist, activist, community worker, or engaged citizen—feel that, like Lalo, you are not alone.

This is the story of the VIVA! project, a transnational exchange that explores stories in their deepest sense. As Cherokee scholar/storyteller Thomas King suggests, "Stories are all that we are; we can't understand ourselves or the world around us without telling a story."[1] Our project questions *who* tells stories, *about what* and *for whom*, *when* and *where*, *why* and *how*, and *in what form*. Stories of "struggle and hope," in the words of Chilean poet Pablo Neruda.[2] Within these pages are the stories of eight community arts projects in five countries; and woven around them, the story of how the VIVA! project created a space for these stories to be shared and probed. How we connected across borders, inspiring and challenging ourselves, each other, and our community organizations, educational institutions, and social movements.

Who is VIVA?

The VIVA! project is a transnational[3] exchange and collaborative research project with eight partners: NGOs and universities in Panama, Nicaragua, Mexico, the United States, and Canada. The NGO partners in Mexico

and Central America are the key popular education centers in their respective countries, with more than four decades of engagement in local, regional, and transnational social movements: the Mexican Institute for Community Development (IMDEC) in Guadalajara and the Panamanian Social Education and Action Center (CEASPA). In Canada, the community partners include the Catalyst Centre, Jumblies Theatre, and the Personal Legacy project. The university partnerships are built on institutional links and with scholars/artists/activists in the Intercultural Communications Institute of URACCAN University in Nicaragua, in the Social Communications Department of the Universidad Autónoma Metropolitana in Mexico City, in the Artsbridge program of the UCLA School of Arts and Architecture in Los Angeles, and in York University's Faculty of Environmental Studies and its Community Arts Practice Program (a joint certificate program of the Faculties of Environmental Studies and Fine Arts).

The projects examined here challenge conventional notions of art as elitist, individual, market driven, or focused solely on form. Whether with Kuna children in Panama recovering cultural and ecological values through traditional music and dances or Somali women sewing

A trajinera or decorated gondola on the canals of Xochimilco, Mexico

Grafitti protesting the massacre in Atenco, Chiapas, Mexico

Spiral symbol of VIVA! project

and singing in a Toronto community center, these initiatives promote the integration of art in its infinite cultural forms into daily rituals, community building, and movements for social change. They uncover hidden stories and offer other ways of telling stories, to counter the official stories fed us by mass media and dominant culture.

Why VIVA?

"Viva!" is a call to memory and to action; it offers a thread between the past and the future. In Spanish it literally means "Long live!" Rooted in Latin American struggles, the cry often recalls past leaders or martyrs and movements while inspiring future collective action. It reminds us that we are part of a longer historical process. "Viva!" is understood in both Spanish and English, reflecting the cross-fertilization of activists in the South and the North. It connotes the fullness of life that is nurtured by cultural action and creative artistic practices in communities. It signals critical hope.

In December of 2006, some of our partners in the VIVA! project were together at a Zapatista gathering of Indigenous communities in the southern Mexican state of Chiapas, organized to show solidarity with the victims of state violence in recent conflicts in Atenco and Oaxaca.[4] As we joined the crowds in shouting, "Viva the victims of Atenco—Viva!" and "Viva the free media—Viva!," the name of our project took on a much more profound and serious connotation; in contexts where peoples' land and livelihood, identity and dignity are under attack, "Viva!" is a cry of life-and-death struggles.

In our cross-border exchange of popular educators and community artists, we came to recognize that this work is more risky in some places than in others. As a Mexican youth activist emphasized: "The difficult situation in Mexico where there is now institutionalized repression, means that people doing alternative media, art, community work, and university-based protests are being persecuted." Some of our partners, for example, have been imprisoned for facilitating community murals or autonomous media. This makes the VIVA! project even more important as a space for critique and solidarity.

How VIVA? Spiraling through Time and Space

The spiral, reflected in the conch shell and snail shell,[5] emerged as a symbol of the VIVA! project after our first year of collaboration. It counters the idea of history as a straight line always moving upward toward some Western notion of progress. It also reflects the dynamic movement of projects and of the exchange among projects, becoming more grounded in local struggles while also reaching out to connect through transnational alliances.

While this book focuses on eight local projects, those projects have been fed by the gatherings that brought us together over years of collaboration. Since April 2003, we have had four exchanges—first in Toronto, Canada, to conceive the project (2003) and to launch it (2004), then in Achiote, Panama (2005), to share and systematize our local projects, and finally, in Chiapas, Mexico (2006), to deepen our collective analysis and consolidate our collective products—a website, book, and videos. Each year we expanded our gatherings to include young participants from the local projects of VIVA! partners.

While we began with one framework—the exploration of creative tensions of community arts and popular education—new questions and frames emerged as we probed our own and each others' practices. This collective theorizing resulted in a spiral-model understanding of our process as well as a decolonizing of our work. The theoretical influences on our thinking are examined in the introduction to this volume.

The accompanying DVD is to be viewed along with this text. The first of the nine videos introduces the VIVA! Project and partners as well as the key ideas shaping our

Laura Reinsborough and José Angel Colman at VIVA! Exchange in Chiapas, Mexico, 2006

Videotaping for BilwiVision in Bilwi, Nicaragua

dialogue over the years. The other eight videos produced by partners bring alive the contexts, participants, and artistic practices of the eight projects examined in these pages. The reader is taken on a visual journey from the Caribbean coast of Nicaragua and Panama to the high rises of suburban Toronto. The protagonists not only celebrate these grassroots initiatives but they reflect on the tensions inevitable in this kind of work.

The core of the book and the DVD, grounding us in the diverse contexts and five countries we represent, is found in the eight chapters that reflect on the community arts projects we analyzed at our annual gatherings. They are put in dialogue with each other under three sections: Recovering Cultural Histories, Transforming Urban Spaces, and Community-University Collaborations.

In Part I, Recovering Cultural Histories: From Indigenous to Diasporic Contexts, we begin with two projects, the Kuna Children's Art Workshops in Panama and the Personal Legacy project in Canada, moving from the southernmost tip of our exchange to its most northern point, from a rural to an urban context. They offer different approaches to recovering history, a process that is central to community arts practice, especially in a global culture that pretends to be ahistorical, while privileging certain cultural histories and worldviews. Communities

who have been historically excluded are reclaiming their own stories and creating their own ways of telling stories.

Between 1993 and 2000, Kuna communities off the Atlantic Coast of Panama involved children in a diverse range of cultural activities, using painting, theater, dance, music, song and poetry, to recover cultural values and promote ecological awareness. As Jesús Alemancia relates in "Planting Good Seeds: The Kuna Children's Art Workshops," these activities were in sharp contrast to the formal school system, which reproduced dominant culture and buried Kuna culture.

Canadian theater artist Diane Roberts, currently artistic director of urban ink productions in Vancouver, British Columbia, responded to a similar dynamic in the north, seeking to "dig up the bones" of the hidden histories of diasporic populations in Canada. In "The Lost Body: Recovering Memory—A Personal Legacy," Diane reflects on this process, which draws from West/Central African dance and story traditions to involve artists in probing their ancestral histories. This project involves people from diverse cultural origins in probing their own embodied memories, a process that is at the same time profoundly personal and implicitly political.

Community arts processes and products have the potential to reclaim and transform public space, countering

The dock at Carti Sugdup, island in Kuna Yala region, Panama

both a diminishing of public space and a sense of alienation many feel in large cities throughout the Americas, which have become the destination of increasing South-North and rural-urban migration. Part II, Transforming Urban Spaces: From Postcolonial Neighborhoods to Public Squares, offers three projects that are creating new cultural fusions of expression and action in Canada and Mexico.

In "Out of the Tunnel There Came Tea: Jumblies Theatre's Bridge of One Hair Project," Ruth Howard and her artistic partners describe how one Toronto neighborhood is being transformed through a three-year community arts process initiated by Jumblies Theatre and involving over thirty artists and hundreds of residents. Informed by the British community play movement, the Bridge of One Hair project has engaged many artists and

residents in a culturally diverse west-end Toronto social housing development in exploring diverse histories, identities, and bridges across their differences.

In 2005–2006, the Catalyst Centre in Toronto brought together artist educators from diverse origins for a popular education train-the-trainer process that led them to design and facilitate projects with diasporic youth to explore and express their stories in many different artistic forms. In "Telling Our Stories: Training Artists to Engage with Communities," Christine McKenzie reflects on the impact of short-term training programs in preparing community artists with popular education skills.

Moving south to Mexico, Leonardo David de Anda Gonzalez and Sergio Eduardo Martínez Mayoral describe another process of reclaiming public space in "A Melting Pot Where Lives Converge: Tianguis Cultural

Mabelle social housing in Etobicoke, Toronto, Canada

de Guadalajara." Organized sixteen years ago by activist youth in Guadalajara, Mexico, Tianguis Cultural weekly draws over two hundred exhibitors (countercultural youth, Indigenous and solidarity groups, NGOs, artists of all kinds) and six thousand visitors to a cultural marketplace that offers a safe space for alternative urban identities and a noncommercial forum for interaction among groups that share a progressive social vision. But it is also a contested space with the conservative municipal government pressuring for a more commercial enterprise.

Finally, the VIVA! Project itself has been a model of collaboration between academic and community partners, finding common ground in their vision of a more just and sustainable world, and democratizing the process of research to honor and draw upon community-based and popular knowledges. Part III thus explores Community-University Collaborations: Blurring the Boundaries.

In Mexico, the Metropolitan Autonomous University in Mexico City has developed a long-term collaboration with Indigenous communities in the southern state of Chiapas. In 2005, social communications professor Sergio

Center for Traditional Medicine and Community Development, URACCAN University, Bilwi, Nicaragua

G. Valdez Ruvalcaba piloted a five-week course-based diploma program in mural production, followed by a year of field work in diverse communities. In "Painting by Listening: Participatory Community Mural Production," Valdez articulates the history and underlying principles of this training program for young artists / animators, which is extending a unique process of mural production that comes from the people themselves and has been applied in communities from the Zapatista autonomous communities to Munich, Germany.

Meanwhile, in cosmopolitan Los Angeles, the ArtsBridge program out of UCLA involves students in arts education residencies with inner-city schools in Los Angeles, nurturing the creativity of the diverse student bodies, cultivating mutually beneficial, respectful, and responsive relationships between the schools, community arts centers, and UCLArts. Amy Shimshon-Santo describes the challenge of facilitating university-community links and creating spaces for marginalized youth to reinvent themselves through art in her chapter, "Connecting the Dots: Linking Schools and Universities Through the Arts."

In the final case study, Margarita Antonio and Reyna Armida Duarte offer the story of BilwiVision in "With Our Images, Voices, and Cultures: BilwiVision—A Community Television Channel." BilwiVision is developing through URACCAN University an alternative practice of communications to reflect the cultural diversity of the Caribbean Coast of Nicaragua through their voices and images. A group of young people of Miskitu, Afri-Caribbean, and Mestizo origins move around the region with small video cameras gathering stories that are drawn from the daily lives of coastal peoples, in contrast to the Hollywood images dominating the satellite offerings. Their participatory research feeds dialogue among coastal peoples about the issues facing them and connects to the mission of URACCAN, a university that is central to the region's autonomy movement.

Community-university collaborations also figure strongly in the short epilogue, "Critical Hope." Two examples of collaboration are highlighted: one from the North and one from the South. The Community Arts Practice (CAP) Certificate at York University in Toronto represents the first university-based training program in the field in

Canada, but experiences the impact of neoliberal policies shaping all universities, with diminishing support for the humanities, arts, and social sciences in a market-driven curriculum. It is contrasted with the proposed integration of the arts and culture into the entire curriculum of URACCAN University in Nicaragua, stimulated by conversations among faculty members at the Fourth VIVA! Encounter held on the Caribbean Coast in the spring of 2010. VIVA! international partners updated us on the projects described in this book, and the Spanish edition of this book was launched. We ask how we can nurture "critical hope" in these contexts, and what is necessary to move these projects forward against tremendous odds.

A Personal Note

As the coordinator of the VIVA! project and coordinating editor of this collection, I have experienced this collaborative research and production process as the culmination of over thirty years of cross-fertilization of education and artistic practices with partners in Central America. Since the late 1970s, Canadians have learned from and supported the innovative popular education movement in the southern hemisphere; we have worked in solidarity with two of the VIVA! partners (IMDEC and CEASPA) for over three decades. At the same time that I have witnessed the political shifts in the Americas from the 1960s to 2010, I have participated in the critical reflection and reinvention of practices, as they have been challenged both from outside forces (from revolutionary to neoliberal agendas) as well as from inside (from Marxist to postmodern, feminist, and Indigenous perspectives). It is in the spirit of popular education to continually reflect on these shifting forces, to respond to each new moment in fresh ways, and to be critically self-reflexive; this is the nature of praxis and the role of creativity and imagination that the arts bring to the challenge.

To guide the reader through fields that may be new to them, a glossary is included at the end of the book. For those who want to be in touch with the organizations whose work is represented here, we offer a list of VIVA! partners and their contacts.

Acknowledgments

It seems incongruous to be holed up in a library carrel writing about the cast of thousands who have contributed to this book. It would feel more appropriate to go out into the streets and break into a *Mama Mia*–type political song and dance with the masses! The human energies behind the projects described in these pages are fueled not only by critical thinking but also by creative experimentation and the tapping of all aspects of our selves—body, mind, and spirit. More importantly, the processes have been collaborative and communal; yet here I sit, alone, in the final stages of the project. Perhaps that is appropriate, as the project began as a dream in my mind, and after spinning off in many serendipitous forms, shaped by many hands, it has returned to me, to pull it together in its final form on my own.

Our original idea was to fill the inside covers of this book with the names of the hundreds who have contributed to the local projects and the transnational meetings, to the funding and to the feeding, to the collective analysis and the often collaborative writing, to the photos and videos, to the feedback and editing, to the reorganizing and the design of the chapters.

So I will try to honor each of these processes by naming the people whose passion, skill, and commitment have made VIVA! live and thrive.

Funders of the research: Social Science and Humanities Research Council of Canada; York University's Faculty of Environmental Studies; York International; York University Vice-President Research and Innovation; Ford Foundation (Mexico City and New York City); CEASPA (Panama); Universidad Autónoma Metropolitana (Mexico City); URACCAN University (Nicaragua).

Publisher: State University of New York Press: Larin McLaughlin, editorial consultant; Laurie Searl, production editor.

Research Collaborators: Deborah Barndt (York, Community Arts Practice); Ruth Howard (Jumblies Theatre); Pato Esquivel, Luis Fernando Gutierrez Araña, Efrén Orozco (IMDEC); Leonardo David de Anda Gonazalez, Sergio Eduardo (Lalo) Martínez Mayoral (Tianguis Cultural); Margarita Antonio, Reyna Armida Duarte (URRACAN, BilwiVision);

VIVA! team meeting in Toronto, Canada in October 2004

VIVA! team meeting in Achiote, Panama in 2005

Jesus Alemancia, Jose Angel Colman, Laura Reinsborough (CEASPA, Proyecto del Arte Kuna); Diane Roberts, Heather Hermant (Personal Legacy project); Christine McKenzie (Catalyst Centre, Telling Our Stories); Sergio G. (Checo) Valdez Ruvalcaba (UAM, Pintar Obedeciendo).

Book Editors: Deborah Barndt (coordinating editor of chapters and introductory chapters); Valerie Miller (editor of English edition); Raúl Leis (editor of Spanish edition); Maggie Hutcheson (review of English edition); Amy Shimshon-Santo (editorial committee member); Sergio G. (Checo) Valdez Ruvalcaba (editorial committee member).

Research and Graduate Assistants: Janna Gorham (2010); Andie Shabbar (2009–2010); Lisa Campbell (2007); Gabrielle Etcheverry (2004); Maggie Hutcheson (2004–2006); Amanda Montgomery (2004–2005); Laura Reinsborough (2005–2006).

Book and Video Translators: Belkis Barrios; Deborah Barndt; Maria Constanza Guzmán; Rita Camacho; Lisa Campbell; Monica Gutierrez; Sylvia Irias-Diaz; Rodrigo Herra; Maggie Hutcheson; Mayahuel Tecozautla.

Glossary: Janna Gorham, Deborah Barndt.

Formatting: Andie Shabbar, Kim Jackson, Tiffany Lord, Glenda Lowndes.

Photo Editing: Joshua Barndt, Deborah Barndt.

Index: Joan Eadie.

VIVA! team meeting in Chiapas, Mexico in 2006

Video Production and Editing: Maggie Hutcheson (overview video and Jumblies video); Pato Esquivel (overview video and Tianguis video); Lisa Campbell (Artsbridges video); Heather Hermant (UAM video); Loreto Bravo, Edie Steiner (Catalyst video); Laura Reinsborough, Deborah Barndt (CEASPA video); Aracelly Duarte and the BilwiVision team, Deborah Barndt (URACCAN video); John Vainstein (video editing assistance).

Video Subtitling: Deborah Barndt; Maggie Hutcheson; Lisa Campbell; Joe the Editor.

Drawings: Margie Adam / ArtWork.

Bilwi Vision staff videotaping in Tuapi, Nicaragua, 2010

Photographs (see photo credits at the end of this volume): Janie Aydin Ali; Deborah Barndt; Loreto Bravo; Katherine Fleitas; Heather Hermant; Joyce Lin; Mario del Monte Martinez; Monique Mojica; Amanda Montgomery; Gerardo Morván Enriques; Amitis Motavelli; Darren O'Donnell; Diane Roberts; Gerardo Rodriguez, Amy Shimshon-Santo; Kara Springer; Sergio G. (Checo) Valdez Ruvalcaba.

Spanish Edition Publishers: URACCAN (Nicaragua).

Research collaborators: IMDEC/Tianguis Cultural: Pato Esquivel; Luis Fernando Arana Gutierrez; David De Anda González; Sergio Eduardo (Lalo) Martínez Mayoral.

CEASPA/ Talleres del Arte Infantil Kuna: Jesús Alemancia; José Angel Colman; Jorge Ventocilla; Blas López; Raúl Leis; Mariela Arce; Laura Reinsborough.

URACCAN/ BilwiVision: Margarita Antonio; Aracelly Reyna Duarte; Monica Gutierrez.

Catalyst Centre/ Telling Our Stories: Christine McKenzie, jin huh (project coordinators); Artist Educators: Mireya Escalante; Rosina Kazi; Lady Noize aka Nylda Gallardo Lopez; Theology 3 aka Theo Steryannis; Saidah Babha Talibah; Darren O'Donnell; Shannon Kitchings; Pasha McKinley. Sponsors: Laidlaw Foundation; Ontario Arts Council; Catalyst Centre; Shakil Choudhury/Brown Book Productions.

The Personal Legacy project: Diane Roberts; Heather Hermant; Lopa Sircar.

Jumblies Theatre: Ruth Howard; Noah Kenneally; Catherine Campbell; Faye Dupras; Loree Lawrence; Margo Charlton; Maggie Hutcheson.

Artistic Team for Bridge of One Hair: Ruth Howard (artistic director/concept creator/shaper/writer/designer);

Erika del Carmen Fuchs translating for VIVA! Exchange in Chiapas, Mexico, 2006

Alice Ping Yee Ho (composer); Hawa Jibril, Duke Redbird (poets); Faduma Ahmed Alim (translator of Somali poems and cultural guide); Faye Dupras (director and dramaturge); Erna Van Daele (musical director); Penny Couchie (choreographer); Noah Kenneally (assistant designer and director); Lisa Marie DiLiberto (assistant director, Metcalf Foundation intern); Trevor Schwellnus (lighting and co-set designer); Loree Lawrence (installation designer, youth arts specialist); Clea Minaker (puppet and props designer); Day Milman (projections designer); Angela Thomas (associate costume designer); Marianne Alas (fabric artist and costume-maker); Performers: Faduma Nkruma, Joqli, Zeinab Labadhagax (Somali musicians), Diana Tso (a professional actor), Shadya Yasin (spoken-word artist and student of York's Community Arts Program), Renwick Herry (Caribbean drummer), Kristin Meuller-Heaslip and Mark Daboll (opera-trained solo singers), VIVA! Youth Singers (an established Toronto choir), Joy Douglas and Wanda Krane (community members).

Funders of Toronto–based projects: Social Investment Fund (TCHC); Ontario Trillium Foundation; Canada Council of the Arts; Ontario Arts Council; Toronto Arts Council; City of Toronto Festivals and Culture Division; Theatre Ontario; Harbourfront Centre; Laidlaw Foundation; United Way of Greater Toronto; New Horizons for Seniors; Metcalf Foundation; Harbinger Foundation; Lawrence Family Foundation; J. P. Bickell Foundation, Raptor's Foundation; John McKellar Foundation; Job Connect; Ontario Works; and private donors.

University of California Los Angeles, Artsbridge: Amy Shimshon-Santo; Lisa Campbell; Vera Caldas.

UAM, Painting by Listening: Sergio (Checo) Valdez Ruvalcaba; Nancy Zuniga; Loreto Bravo; Sabina Schratzenstaller; Heather Hermant; Alex Goss.

Proposal Development Workshop (Toronto, Canada, 2003): Deborah Barndt; Danny Caldan; Chris Cavanagh; Luis Fernando Araña Gutierrez; Ileana Lacayo; Christine McKenzie; John Vainstein; Checo Valdez; Rebecca Santiago; Eduardo Tinkam.

First Team Meeting Participants (Toronto, Canada, 2004): Jesús Alemancia; Deborah Barndt; Pato Esquivel; Christine McKenzie; Efrén Orozco; Checo Valdez; Amanda Montgomery (interpreter); Lee Bensted (interpreter); Alice Johnson (interpreter); Petra Kukacka (interpreter).

Harvesting Stories Conference (October 2004): Organizers: Deborah Barndt; Chris Cavanagh; Gabrielle Etcheverry; Maggie Hutcheson; Christine McKenzie; Amanda Montgomery.

Popular Education Elders and Storytellers: Jesus Alemancia; Bev Burke; Chris Cavanagh; Pato Esquivel; Leesa Fawcett; Honor Ford-Smith; Bob Henderson; Carl James; Tina Lopes; D'Arcy Martin; Valerie Miller; Eduardo Tinkham Moody; Denise Nadeau; Efrén Orozco; Barb Thomas; Lynne Davis; Sergio G. Valdez Ruvalcaba.

Second Team Meeting Participants (Achiote, Panama, 2005): Jesús Alemancia; Leonardo David de Anda Gonzalez; Margarita Antonio; Deborah Barndt; Loreto Bravo; Danny Caldan; Margo Charlton; Dagoberto Chung; Anselmo Cooper; Carlos Darinel Domínguez; Charlotte Elton; Pato Esquivel; Heather Hermant; Lil Herrera (interpreter); Raúl Leis; José Luis Lora; Christine McKenzie; Amanda Montgomery (interpreter); Efrén Orozco; Laura Reinsborough; Diane Roberts; Gabriela Rodríguez Arribau; Amy Shimshon-Santo; Yerka Soleado; Checo Valdez; Herberto Valdes P.; Jorge Ventocilla.

Third Team Meeting Participants (Chiapas, Mexico, 2006): Margarita Antonio; Loreto Bravo; Lisa Campbell;

VIVA! partners are served by kitchen staff of Universidad de la Tierra in Chiapas, Mexico, 2006

José Angel Colman; Reyna Armida Duarte; Pato Esquivel; Olmo Flores Mosqueda; Erika Fuchs (interpreter); Luis Fernando Araña Gutierrez; Heather Hermant; Rodrigo Herra (interpreter); Maggie Hutcheson; Noah Kenneally; Sergio Eduardo (Lalo) Martínez Mayoral; Christine McKenzie; Laura Reinsborough; Diane Roberts; Sergio G. (Checo) Valdez Ruvalcaba; Rebeca Santiago (interpreter); Sabina Schratzenstaller; Amy Shimshon-Santo; Nancy Zuniga.

Web Design and Maintenance: Lisa Campbell-Salazar; Josué Salazar; Laura Reinsborough; Loreto Bravo; Maggie Hutcheson; Kris Ericson; Deborah Barndt; Herb van den Dool.

York University Administrative Support: Patrick Lacey; Tiffany Lord; Rhoda Reyes; Bev Rutherford.

Drivers: Raulito Leis; Gerardo Rodríguez; Lolo Silva.

Rooted in Place, Politics, Passion, and Praxis

Decolonization, Popular Education, Community Arts, and Participatory Action Research

The central ideas driving the VIVA! project can be seen within a circle that acknowledges our colonial history and aims to decolonize our practice as educators, artists, and activists through popular education, community arts, and participatory action research. In this chapter, I introduce these key fields that provide the common theoretical and methodological ground for the projects described within these pages. The stories you will read are rooted in place, politics, passion, and praxis—four interrelated components that together aim for balance in our practice.[1]

PLACE:
Decolonization

POLITICS:
Popular Education

PRAXIS:
Participatory Action
Research

PASSION:
Community Arts

Rooted in place: The colonial context of the Americas

Every context is political in its own different way, whether it's rooted in your body, or it's rooted in the colonial history of people trying to take back the land that they live on or people who have been displaced from their land and don't know each other in their new community. I see more similarities than differences among our projects in this sense.[2]
—Christine McKenzie, Catalyst Centre
(Canada)

All VIVA! partners and projects are located in multicultural contexts, with Indigenous and diasporic populations from many different origins being central protagonists in

diverse processes of community-based art-making. Our cross-border exchange speaks to an increasingly integrated hemispheric economy that is epitomized by the migration north of many Central Americans, and reflected in the U.S.-controlled global media.

Our exchange is also an example of the globalizing of civil society and a growing movement of Indigenous peoples, communities of color and their allies challenging the "official stories" of dominant media and the Eurocentric values driving corporate globalization.

José Angel Colman, a Kuna popular theater artist in Panama, found that our exchange challenged dominant media stereotypes:

> With the monopoly of global media, we mainly get information from the metropolitan centers. So part of the work of popular education in our communities is to counter that, because we know that even in the U.S., people also struggle to have access to art, to information.

VIVA! partner Nicaraguan journalist Margarita Antonio builds on this idea:

> We see a lot of stereotyped images of the U.S., where everything is idealized, or where everyone is imperialist. But projects like ArtsBridge in Los Angeles show us that even in this world of the big dreams, there is a lot of work going on, there are people who are really the majority, who are constructing something different, and art is the path.
>
> We need a more accurate image of life in the north, recognizing that there are many immigrants from our countries living there. Because these same young people when they return from the U.S. to our communities, they often sell a false image to our youth who think that "this is the life!" and they have to go there, too, when they could be building their lives in their own context.

ArtsBridge director Amy Shimshon-Santo of Los Angeles, speaking from the North, agrees that the VIVA! project reveals the global dynamics of culture.

> To be able to see in Guadalajara's cultural marketplace, for example, a punk artist, an Indig-

enous activist, reflects a different diversity. Still, we recognize that not everyone is equal.

Five hundred years of colonization: Carved in stone?

The issue of power and inequality, in fact, is central to community arts and popular education. Through the VIVA! project, we aimed to unearth the roots of these deeply ingrained power dynamics, a shared colonial history, represented by this statue. A monument of Christopher Columbus with an Indigenous woman at his feet could be located anywhere in the hemisphere or even

Statue of Christopher Columbus and Indigenous woman in Lima, Peru

in Europe. As a catalyst it can help us rethink how we both reflect and reproduce the power relations represented here. We can also critically analyze it as a piece of art: Who constructed it and for whom? This particular statue was erected in Peru in 1867 by a European sculptor as a tribute to the Spanish colonizers. It offers one representation of the colonial history and its deconstruction feeds the postcolonial theoretical framework of the VIVA! project.

The statue immortalizes the white male European "discoverer" who brought "civilization"—epitomized by opulent clothing, a cross, and an upward gaze—to the "savages/heathens," here a naked Indian woman. The military struggle involved in the subjugation is only hinted at by her arrow tossed to the side. Even though this artistic representation is more than 150 years old, people today inevitably still see their own lives within the persistent (carved in stone?) and intersecting power relations represented here: sexism, heterosexism, classism, militarism, evangelization, racism.[3] Both its content and its form say something about Eurocentric ways of knowing and artistic expression. Yet, as Ania Loomba reminds us, there is a danger in reproducing the binary opposites represented in the figures of the colonizer and colonized, even as we attempt to expose how they have functioned historically to

construct the European self and the other.[4] The relation is complex, and there are contradictions within.

Representatives from each of the VIVA! projects see this image through different lenses, depending on their own identities, histories, and locations. As Heather Hermant reflects in the VIVA! video:

> Even within our own group, we see the colonial story repeating itself—in little bursts—all the time, and that in itself speaks to why we need to be doing this kind of work.

No matter where we are located, we have to confront the fact that we are all immersed in colonial contexts that are not just of the past, but perpetuated in new forms such as corporate globalization. Our projects inevitably reflect our locations in the struggle between colonization and decolonization. VIVA! partners respond to this statue from their own vantage points:

José Angel Colman (Panama) was provoked by the image of the cross:

> Since we were born, the Catholic Church was there teaching us the Bible, which was like the

José Angel Colman, Panama

Diane Roberts, Canada

ABCs of another culture. . . . I was brought up as a Christian, but I've come to the conclusion that I'm not a Christian. We Kunas have our own Indigenous religion; through my religion, I can accept the face of Christ as an historical being.

As an Afri-Caribbean woman, Diane Roberts (Canada) asks us to consider who is missing from this official artistic representation of the Americas:

It is impossible to ignore slavery or the slave trade. The river of blood I referred to fed the land, makes the land grow, and mixes with the blood of all of the ancestors in this room. But there is a devaluing of the contribution of the African culture, a deracination, a removing of race, a removing of culture. Yet we can see it in the music, the dance, the literature.

Margarita Antonio (Nicaragua), a Miskitu woman, responds to the gender dynamic in this statue, challenging the image of a subservient Indigenous woman and reflecting on colonization and art:

In Nicaragua, we can see two levels of colonization: first how those of us from the pluriethnic

Margarita Antonio, Nicaragua

Caribbean Coast are seen by the Pacific mestizo (Spanish descendants) side of the country, where we are represented in the news only when there are disasters or drugs. And secondly, how we have internalized this colonized view of ourselves, so we reproduce in our community television station how others see us, for example, focusing on barely clad women dancing.

In working with artists of color who have developed projects with marginalized youth, Christine McKenzie (Canada) raises questions about the ethics of representation:

We can't use photos of the "at risk" youth in our material without their permission or participation, and, similarly, who asked the Indigenous people how they wanted to be represented in this statue? What's more, the Indigenous woman is being sexualized, which is another part of the patriarchal and racist colonizing project.

Rebeca Santiago (Mexico):

We as Mexicans have a continuous colonial process with North America, through its food, its fashion. For example, I work with artisans and I see the artisan dressed up in a Converse baseball cap and running shoes, and a brand-name T-shirt, but he has nothing to feed his wife. We call this "cultural hybridity" in which our culture is subjugated by the colonial culture, by the dominating culture.

Christine McKenzie, Canada

Amy Shimshon-Santo (USA):

These same dynamics exist in the inner-city schools of Los Angeles today, kids in poor and racialized neighborhoods are shaped by homogenous consumer culture, but are denied the resources, the chance to express themselves and their diversity through many other forms, much livelier than monuments, like break dancing.

Noah Kenneally (Canada):

Since Jumblies Theatre proposes working across differences—of race, generation, and class in Toronto—we would challenge the representation limited to only two groups, and ask how bridges could be built between the marginalized groups (Indigenous, African, etc.) as well as with mestizos and creoles in the current context.

Checo Valdez (Mexico), a mestizo graphic artist who critiques his own training in European art as egoistic, says:

Our concepts of art come from Europe; the term "art" itself is colonized.

Amy Shimshon-Santo, U.S.A.

Checo challenges the fact that this statue was produced by a European sculptor, revealing a Eurocentric view of the world, and in a European form, the monument. Through the Painting by Listening project, he facilitates a participatory community mural production process in which people bring their own histories and aesthetics to a mural that they themselves paint.

Deborah Barndt (coordinator, VIVA! project, Canada):

How do we decolonize the VIVA! project itself when it has been initiated in the North, funded by Western academic monies, and coordinated by me, a white Anglo university professor? Every meeting, every written document, every artistic product emerging from this project bears the traces of

Noah Kenneally, Canada

colonization. How can we alert the reader of our book to look critically for those contradictions within these pages?

As the VIVA! project evolved, it became clearer that we were engaged in a process of decolonization: of education, of research, of art, and of community. Examining any one of these practices or constructs inevitably implicates the others; that is, in attempting to decolonize them, we are reclaiming their inseparability. In considering the colonizer–colonized relationship, each of us in the VIVA! project is located in different (and shifting) places in these relationships of power. The challenge is how to acknowledge these differences as we work through them and with them. This is an ongoing process of questioning for all community artists and activists: How

does the Columbus statue reflect your history and current relationships? What is missing? How do we find the cracks within institutions of power to creatively challenge and change unjust power relations?

Digging up the bones: Decolonizing as a conscious process

If none of us escapes the process of colonization, if it continues with or without our participation, with or without our consent, then decolonization is a process that we must enter into consciously. We must choose to participate in it, even within our own interrelationships and find ways to involve others in this process. VIVA! partner Diane Roberts raises questions about the language we use:

Checo Valdez, Mexico

I want to find a way to name it so that it's not hidden, so that we have a language for naming it without it being buried. I'm just trying to find a way to dig up the bones and to be able to look at them.

Decolonization can be seen as comprising several different processes: acknowledging the history of colonialism; working to undo the effects of colonialism; striving to unlearn habits, attitudes, and behaviors that continue to perpetuate colonialism; and challenging and transforming institutional manifestations of colonialism.[5]

Maori scholar Linda Tuhiwai Smith in her classic *Decolonizing Methodologies: Research and Indigenous Peoples* connects colonialism to European imperialism that involved not only economic expansion and the subjugation of "others" but also an idea or spirit as well as a particular field of knowledge.[6] Postcolonial theorists (Fanon,[7] Loomba,[8] Young,[9] Spivak[10]) have helped us unpack colonial notions of knowledge and knowledge production while also probing the ways that colonized peoples are speaking back from the margins, reclaiming not only their land but also diverse ways of knowing and communicating.

In *The Archive and the Repertoire: Performing Cultural Memory in the Americas*, performance theorist Diana Taylor explores the tensions between the Eurocentric text-based ways of knowing and performative practices that honored embodied knowledges. In her genealogy of cultural practices in the Americas, Taylor delineates how colonization involved discrediting Indigenous ways of "preserving and communicating historical understanding."[11] At the same time, the colonizers witnessed the performance of rituals that integrated many forms of artistic expression; for example, they used the Arawack word *areitos* to describe "a collective act involving singing, dancing, celebration, and worship that claimed aesthetic as well as sociopolitical and religious legitimacy," reflecting that the cultural expressions of the Indigenous communities "exceed the compartmentalization, either by genre, by participant-actors, or by intended effect . . . that ground Western cultural thought."[12] We see this privileging of text-based learning over embodied practices in academic contexts and even in our attempts to write about embodied practices in books like this one! While acknowledging this contradiction, we urge the reader to refer regularly to the accompanying videos, which will stimulate the senses and provoke the emotions, through bodies and sound, movement and connection.

Indigenous cultures had no word for art, yet they

Deborah Barndt, coordinator, VIVA! project, Canada

do have names for specific cultural forms, such as the elaborate masks and powerful totem poles of the Haida on the coast of British Columbia that now grace major art museums and are being recognized for how they pass on ancestral knowledge in the context of community ceremonies. In *Look to the Mountain*, Santa Clara Pueblo educator Gregory Cajete frames art as integral to the educative process of the community, based in visions and dreams.[13] There is among Indigenous peoples both a reclaiming of traditional practices as well as a creative fusion of the historical forms with new technologies, and a challenge to the stereotypes of Aboriginals as frozen in the past.[14] For Indigenous peoples, resistance to the imposition of dominant cultures has often meant learning various cultures and developing the capacity to operate in many different contexts, and to construct bridges to support meeting across differences. VIVA! partner Jose Colman refers to his experience with

Kuna children who learned from their elders while also attending Panamanian public school:

> People are dynamic, they aren't static. Indigenous people advance, are sometimes pulled, changes are always coming. I believe that the Kuna Children's Art Workshops were important because they were flexible and run with a spirit of accepting others. We don't see ourselves shaping ourselves only as Indigenous people, in order to close ourselves within our Indigeneity. We are forming ourselves in our own traditional school as Indigenous people in order to project ourselves in the broader world.

Collaborators in the VIVA! project, from the Global North and the Global South, have found many allies in the process of decolonizing our art, education, and research. Ontologically, we critique the materialistic and mechanistic worldview driving global imperialism; epistemologically, we identify with postcolonial notions of knowledge and power; and methodologically, we adopt a feminist poststructural stance that honors the subjective, emotional, aesthetic, and natural.[15] We ally with feminists, Indigenous scholars, critical race theorists, and environmentalists in countering notions of knowledge as static, positivist, and commodified, and in arguing for an epistemology (way of knowing) of multiple perspectives, an understanding of power/knowledge as historically contingent, and an emphasis on the processes rather than the products of research, education, and art.[16]

Ultimately, our goal is not merely anticolonial, it is shaped by a vision that embraces all people, while acknowledging difference. African American scholar/activist Robin D. G. Kelley suggests that the way "to dream ourselves out of this dark place" is "to think like poets (*sic* artists), to envision and make visible a new society, a peaceful, cooperative, loving world without poverty and oppression, limited only by our imaginations."[17]

As U.S.-based educator/artist Amy Shimshon-Santo articulates in the introductory video accompanying this book:

> Decolonization is to come into that awareness of how your ancestors brought you here, and to engage in an affirming way with who you are, where you came from, and what your potential for creativity and change might be. Cultural and educational institutions should be reflective of who we are as a people. What we consider beautiful, what we consider meaningful, what we consider intelligent and knowledgeable, should be reflective of all of us.

Popular education can animate the process of unveiling and transforming power relations, while community arts can tap our collective imaginations about other ways of being. As Myles Horton, renown North American educator, storyteller, and founder of the Highlander Research and Education Center[18] would put it: "We need two eyes: one focused on what is, the other on what could be."[19]

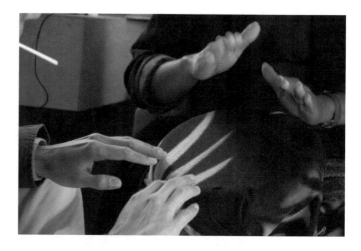

Rooted in politics: Popular education as a common ground

The partnerships at the core of the VIVA! project were forged in the early 1980s when many educators, activists, and artists from all over the Americas converged in Nicaragua, during the early moments of the Sandinista Revolution. The first project of the new government was to mount a National Literacy Crusade that mobilized the entire country for five months, involving over 100,000 volunteers (a majority young urban students) in teaching reading and writing to 400,000 illiterate workers and peasants who in turn taught their "teachers" about the realities of their lives.[20] The campaign not only reduced the illiteracy rate from 52 to 12 percent but it transformed people who had been historically marginalized by colonialism and U.S.-supported dictatorships into active participants in the construction of a new society, based on socialist values. Popular education collectives were established in the communities for ongoing education and community development, with the new literates becoming teachers of their neighbors.[21]

I was one of many internationalists who arrived at this historic moment to share technical expertise with the massive educational program. I was invited to teach photography as part of a process of producing curriculum materials based on the stories of the adult learners and their daily lives. Between 1981 and 1983, we trained a team of popular photo journalists to produce a magazine for the new literates and mounted production centers in three regions of the country for teachers and community leaders to produce their own photo stories, silk-screened posters, and theater pieces, all to feed the literacy process. The Nicaraguan Ministry of Education had invited Paulo Freire, renowned Brazilian educator, to advise them on their curriculum and methodology; Freire encouraged educators to develop a model that would fit their context.

The Nicaraguan adult education program in the 1980s strongly reflected Freirean principles of "popular education": that education is not neutral, that it must start with the experiences and perceptions of the learners, that the content should be drawn from their daily lives, that the teachers are learners and learners teachers. Freire framed literacy more broadly as not only learning to read the "word" but also to read the "world"; his problem-posing approach to education drew upon the social contradictions learners faced in their daily lives. While learning to read and write, they discussed their common social conditions and considered how they might act collectively to transform them. This process of "conscientization" integrated the personal and political, the individual and collective, action and reflection (praxis).

Freire built on an analysis of power as articulated by Antonio Gramsci. The Italian Communist journalist offered three concepts critical to the VIVA! project. First, Gramsci introduced the concepts of hegemony and counter-hegemony as a way of understanding power and struggle for change. His notion of hegemony is very dynamic, framing power as relational, or persuasion from above as well as consent from below. Gramsci suggested that dominant groups maintain ideological control through intellectual and moral persuasion, winning the hearts and minds of people who might not even share their interests. Struggles for power by marginalized groups represent "counter-hegemonic" forces that challenge and transform this dominant hegemony.

The late Canadian popular educator, artist, and activist dian marino eloquently interpreted Gramsci and captured hegemony in her own life as "a rainforest of movable relations."[22] Gramsci not only challenged more dogmatic Marxist interpretations of power, by framing power in more fluid and relational, and less deterministic ways, but he also emphasized the importance of the cultural realm to enrich and complexify a political economic analysis. People must consent to dominant ideas and practices in order for hegemony to work. Ideological institutions such as schools and the media are critical to this process, and so any efforts to challenge current power relations must involve processes of education and communication. Popular education and community arts are counter-hegemonic practices within the cultural sphere. Both practices are about engaging minds, hearts, and bodies in transformative processes, which aim to develop critical social consciousness and move toward more collective actions.

Finally, Gramsci offers a more dialectical way of thinking that challenges positivist, linear, and dichotomous ways of framing issues. He proposes naming and engaging contradictions; it is only within the spaces created by contradictions of any given moment that we can take action. The framework of the VIVA! project embraces contradictions in the way that Gramsci advocates. By naming and exploring creative tensions, we acknowledge that they are inherent to community arts practices; they are not necessarily to be resolved but rather to be acknowledged and engaged. At the same time, we have been influenced by feminist, antiracist, and postcolonial critiques that recognize the complexity and intersectionality of power,[23] alerting us to the ways that gender, race, class, sexuality, Indigeneity, and education shape our identities and relationships. While we are indebted to Freire and Gramsci, we also recognize their historical locations and limits;[24] like bell hooks, we are thirsty for their enormous theoretical contributions even if we are drinking "dirty water."[25]

Having studied Freire's methodology in Peruvian literacy programs in the 1970s,[26] I was aware that popular education emerged out of the grassroots struggles of poor communities throughout Latin America, in response to the military dictatorships, U.S. intervention, and neocolonial development programs. Freire brilliantly conceptualized that practice and, especially after he was exiled in the 1960s, became a major theorist of an emerging pedagogy of the oppressed (also the title of his classic text).[27] Of particular interest to me was Freire's suggestion that images or theater or songs or any cultural expression could serve as codes representing a common social reality and could be engaged or decoded by learners to deepen their critical consciousness of their situation. Popular art and communications were integral to popular education from the start.

In Nicaragua, I found a gathering of internationalist popular educators who had been applying Freirean notions to their own contexts across the continents. While many were invited as educational consultants, they also found their own theoretical and practical understanding deepened and broadened by the revolutionary moment in Nicaragua, with a government that prioritized popular education for the historically marginalized. Out of those relationships, in fact, the ALFORJA network was formed, a loose alliance of six major popular education centers in six Central American countries.[28]

Over the next three decades the ALFORJA network inspired by those dynamic years in Nicaragua, provided the most fertile ground for the theoretical and methodological development of popular education.[29] They organized annual ten-day Creativity Workshops in which popular educators from the region reflected critically on their practice and collectively tackled critical social issues, developed sophisticated methodologies, and dreamed up creative and dynamic participatory techniques.[30] The "dialectical methodology of popular education," for example, conceptualized in detail the movement from practice to theory and back to practice; it has been adapted by North American popular educators in a spiral model for designing educational events, which also "starts with the experience and knowledge of participants, identifies patterns in their stories, adds new information (theory) to what they already know, practices skills, and then strategically applies what's been learned in the world."[31]

Two of the major centers in the network are current VIVA! partners, the Panamanian Social Education and Action Center (CEASPA) and the Mexican Institute for Community Development (IMDEC). CEASPA was known in the 1980s for its groundbreaking research on national issues, its magazine *Diálogo Social*, and a monthly gathering of social activists undertaking a "conjunctural analysis" of current events and plotting strategic coalitional actions. This latter practice inspired The Moment Project at the Jesuit Centre for Social Faith and Justice (1985–1995), resulting in a Canadian version of political analysis for action, which we called "naming the moment."[32]

The Mexican Institute for Community Development (IMDEC), located in Guadalajara, Mexico, has for forty-five years been the key national training ground for popular educators, community organizers, and social movement activists. IMDEC staff developed a four-week methodological school in popular education and pioneered a process of *sistematización*, which helps groups extract the key learnings from their organizational practices and collective actions.[33] IMDEC has also been the key leader in the network in the field of popular communications, promoting the democratization of art and media and their use in popular education and grassroots organizing. IMDEC has produced dozens of videos and books, and has offered communications training in community radio, video, photography, and print media.[34]

Central American popular educators have had a huge influence on the development of the field in North America as well as in Europe.[35] In Canada, ALFORJA members came north to help us establish the Doris Marshall Institute for Education and Action (1985–1995); similar work has been carried on since the late 1990s by the Catalyst Centre, one of the VIVA! partners.[36] Of the other VIVA! partners, teachers in the two universities in Mexico and in Nicaragua were more familiar with popular education, given its influence in the region, than those in the North. York University, however, the host of the project, for over twenty years offered the only graduate course in Canada in popular education for social change.

In the adoption of popular education in the North, there has always been a danger that it is reduced to participatory techniques and depoliticized, while its origins and intent have been intensely political; there is also an important debate about the application of these methods with more privileged populations.[37] Paulo Freire has had an influence in the academy in the related field of critical pedagogy (Giroux, McLaren, Shor, and Simon),[38] which has tended to focus more on the application of his ideas in public schools, while popular education as a practice in social movements has been adapted in the women's movement,[39] antiracism movement,[40] environmental movement,[41] antiglobalization movement,[42] and progressive sectors of the labor movement.[43] Thirty years ago, the term was unfamiliar to those in the North, equated with pop culture, rather than understood as the Spanish "popular," which has a class connotation in Latin America, referring to the people, the grassroots, or most marginalized populations.

When VIVA! partners first gathered in 2004 to collectively shape our project, we nonetheless agreed that popular education was our common ground, and a starting point. Our objectives focused on two levels of activity:

A local objective: Using participatory action research, to recover, promote, and create diverse cultural and artistic practices integrated into processes of popular education and community organization, and aimed at both personal and social transformation that respects diversity.

A transnational objective: Through gatherings, workshops, videos, and books, to organize exchanges of practices and theories, promoting a critical and self-critical perspective and strengthening multicultural and transnational solidarity.

In our first meeting, while we agreed that popular education was common to our practices, we had diverse ways of defining it. From Panama, Kuna educator and CEASPA director Jesús Alemancia described it as "the act of educating and being educated, of enriching 'knowing' by participating in the processes of life (social, economic, political, cultural and individual)," while Christine McKenzie of the Toronto-based Catalyst Centre defined popular education as "grassroots people collectively raising consciousness, analyzing their histories and current situation, and from this acting to challenge unjust power that affects their social realities."[44]

Since the 1994 implementation of the North American Free Trade Agreement and the Zapatista uprising challenging the impact of neoliberal corporate globalization on lands and peoples, biodiversity and cultural diversity, there has also been a concomitant globalization of social movements. Popular educators, social justice activists, and committed artists have been responding to similar forces of privatization, deregulation, a diminishing of the public and social sphere; geopolitical borders have become less relevant as they find ways of connecting through social media and new technologies such as mobile phones.[45] These tools have also become part of our exchange, and have shaped our constantly evolving frameworks.[46]

Popular education itself has been challenged for its Eurocentrism, evident in its Marxist intellectual roots, a rationalist orientation, and a focus on class often at the expense of questions of race, gender, and sexuality. Postcolonial and postmodern critiques have reshaped the theoretical frames and strategic directions of popular educators.[47] Raul Leís, VIVA! partner in Panama and secretary general of CEEAL, Latin American Council for Adult Education, offered this conjunctural assessment at our 2005 gathering:

Popular education now faces new challenges, it is time to revitalize our practice. For example, before the focus was the working class, now it is social movements. In the past, we focused on what we considered "objective reality," now we also pay attention to the "subjective." Before we had socialism as a utopia, but then the [Berlin] wall fell. Now we have to build the kind of world we want, not based on dogma. We have to cultivate, sow, and water it to make it grow. And, as Paulo Freire would say, dialogue remains the core of our action, dialogue even with our contradictions.

Leis concludes:

In Latin America, popular education and popular theater can help build critical hope through a collective and participatory process of change. Independent of ideologies. That is, we cannot support a libratory proposal that is authoritarian, that would be a contradiction in terms. A transformative methodology must be ethical as well as political.

Rooted in passion: Community arts as a common strategy[48]

At the core of the VIVA! project is a belief in the power of the arts and a commitment to reclaiming the right and capacity of everyone to express themselves, their identities, concerns, hopes, and visions through a myriad of cultural forms. For many of us, this is what has been missing in top-down, didactic, and text-heavy approaches to education and organizing by leaders of progressive social movements.

Community arts, as a term and recognized field of practice, only came into currency in the latter part of the twentieth century. But the process it refers to—the engagement of people in representing their collective identities, histories, and aspirations in multiple forms of expression—is as old as cave paintings and ritualistic chanting. Gregory Cajete describes art in North American Aboriginal contexts as "an expression of life" practiced by all the people, usually an "anonymous activity expressing a unique cultural perspective of living."[49] Thus, art was/ is integral to life, totally democratized, and reflecting a community rather than an individual identity. Art was/ is also a means of visioning, used within rituals and ceremonies, and integrating "myth, dream, art, ecological philosophy, communality, and spirit."[50] Certainly for many Aboriginal peoples art is synonymous with community, whereas for the mainstream Western art world, "community art" is often discredited as something of lesser quality when judged against the work of individual geniuses of "high art."

The separation of "art" from "community" perhaps has its roots in both a body/mind and a nature/culture split in Western consciousness emerging from certain streams of the European scientific revolution of the 1700s[51] and in the commodification of art and knowledge associated with industrial capitalism of the 1800s.[52] This has intensified in recent decades with commercialized and individualistic practices of art and media in the context of corporate cultural globalization, often "reducing culture to commerce."[53] This process is paralleled by and integral to the commodification of knowledge, which emphasizes knowledge transmission and accumulation rather than the knowledge production process, and frames learning as a personal and primarily mental undertaking rather than a social relation and holistic experience.[54]

Besides the resistance of Aboriginal peoples to fragmented ways of knowing often implicitly promoted in Western schools, media, and institutions, there have been many forms of education, art, and activism that have also challenged these dominant paradigms.[55] In the North American context, the cultural workers of the 1930s, for example, promoted collective production of the arts through the mural movement and film, theater, and dance workers' leagues associated with socialist politics and supported by U.S. President Roosevelt's New Deal programs.[56] Community development and community animation in the radical 1960s (and the related *animation socioculturelle* in Quebec) linked the organizing of marginalized communities with the expression of their issues through theater (Teatro Campesino was linked to organizing Chicano farmworkers in California[57]), video (the Canadian National Film Board's Challenge for Change program documented and represented video portraits back to Maritimes communities[58]), and music (Black spirituals were transformed into hymns of the United States–based civil rights movement[59]).

In the Latin American context, popular communications was a more common term than community arts, and, along with popular education, was integral to the building of social movements in the 1960s and 1970s to challenge military dictatorships, United States intervention, and extreme disparities between the rich and the poor in the southern hemisphere.[60] Art and media forms such as community radio, popular theater, *nueva canción* (new song), slide shows, and video were democratized and used to engage an exploited majority in naming and challenging current power relations while envisioning utopias of more just and equitable societies.[61] In this context, the critical and the creative were wed. As popular education promoted the collective production of knowledge, popular art offered both a mode of collective inquiry and a form of communicating that knowledge to the poor majority in ways that touched hearts as well as minds. It was understood that change would not happen unless the majority not only understood the root causes of their oppression and the necessity of struggle but also felt a deep commitment to working for change and a growing sense of their own power to make a difference.

The arts were not only tools in education and organization but engaged people more fully, moved their spirits, and inspired collective action. In the past twenty years, the term "community arts" has become more common in North America, but its meaning remains as diverse as the contexts in which it is practiced. At its most conservative, it refers to the dissemination of elite or classical arts to rural communities that have been marginalized by the large (and more heavily funded) urban cultural centers. Many municipal or provincial community arts councils, for example, were responses to this disparity. Adams and Goldbard, U.S. consultants in community arts for the past thirty years, eschew the term because of this connotation and prefer instead the concept of community cultural development, which they define as "a range of initiatives undertaken by artists in collaboration with other community members to express identity, concerns and aspirations through the arts and communications media, while building cultural capacity and contributing to social change."[62]

Until late 2010, a community arts website based in Virginia provided a gathering place, a rich collection of readings, and an exchange of artistic projects in fields ranging from corrections, education, environment, health, and spirituality.[63] One section listed over one hundred opportunities for training in community arts in North America, from courses or degrees in arts, urban studies, and education to summer institutes offered by established socially relevant art groups. The teaching of art for social change was a rallying point for progressive artists and academics meeting at the College Art Association conference in Los Angeles in 2009, where Beverly Naidus's *Teaching Outside the Frame: Art for Social Change*[64] was

launched and incorporated the practice of over twenty artists/activists/educators. Thus, the field is growing, even as funding sources have diminished.

In the Canadian context, this new institutional space, however, has also been claimed by more political artists, who work collaboratively with diverse communities of interest and location. Honor Ford-Smith, Jamaican Canadian theater artist and postcolonial theorist, assesses both the potential and the dangers revealed in a new surge of public and private funding for community arts. Concerned that funders might hijack community agendas, she argues for an increasingly hybrid definition of community and community arts, one that allows for a diversity of practice, that promotes rigorous critique of all practice, and that challenges the essentially conservative dichotomy between professional and amateur and between product and process.[65] Among activists of the new millennium, there has also been a resurgence of participatory production of the arts, often in response to the commodified culture of global capitalism and the promotion of passive consumption rather than active citizenship.[66] It is evident in the proliferation of puppets, masks, and performance artists in street protests,[67] as well as in the adoption of culture-jamming practices,[68] theater of the oppressed techniques,[69] hip hop music, and reclaim the streets movements.[70] It is perhaps most fertile currently in creative activist art blossoming from multiple sites through new social media[71] and web-based activisms.[72]

Community arts is often implicitly a critique of the domination of Western mass media and popular consumer culture. It is also a response to migration and diasporic populations claiming and creating diverse and multiple identities. In global cities such as Toronto, a cauldron of diverse cultural practices, new cultural fusions are drawing on traditions that challenge the Eurocentric content and individualism of hegemonic White Western culture.[73]

In using the term "community arts" in the VIVA! project, then, we recognize its multiple connotations and the contestations about who does it, in what contexts, for what, and how. The juxtaposition of the two words—"art" and "community"—challenges our commonsense notions of both complex concepts. It behooves us to constantly interrogate how we understand art (as most of us are socialized in a more colonial and capitalist notion of the term) as well as how we understand community—

whether it be defined by place, tradition, intention, practice, or spirit.

Cleveland suggests that community arts can nurture four different kinds of purposes: to educate and inform us about ourselves and the world; to inspire and mobilize individuals and groups; to nurture and heal people and/or communities; to build and improve community capacity.[74]

The social experience of art-making can open up aspects of people's beings, their stories, their memories and aspirations, in ways that other methods might miss. When people are given the opportunity to tell their own stories—whether through oral traditions, theater, visual arts, music, or other media—they bring their bodies, minds, and spirits into a process of communicating and sharing their experiences; they affirm their lives as sources of knowledge, and they stimulate each other in a synergistic process of collective knowledge production. Art, education, and research become part of the same dynamic and creative process.

Rooted in praxis: Participatory action research as a common methodology

Pure action without reflection is uncritical and nonstrategic activism, while pure reflection without action is mere verbalism.
—Paulo Freire, *Pedagogy of the Oppressed*

Integral to popular education is a process of participatory research, engaging learners in an investigation of their own lives in order to more deeply understand the power relations that limit them so they can become more conscious and active agents of change. Participatory research in fact originated within popular education networks, and is understood to be in-

tegral to the three-pronged process of research, education, and action associated with Freirean-shaped popular education.[75] Community arts and popular communications are thus tools in this process of people researching their own lives.[76] VIVA! partners adapted a participatory action research (PAR) methodology, based on the notion of praxis promulgated by the thought of Freire and Gramsci. We proposed this approach for our case studies, as a way to involve participants of local projects in naming the issues that are most critical to them and their context, in probing them through community arts processes, and in envisioning change and/or feeding social movement action.

According to Kemmis, PAR is critical social research, different from positivist research (often carried out by a detached scientist) or interpretive research (focusing on subjective meanings). The purpose of liberatory or critical research is the creation of movement for personal and social transformation in order to redress injustices, support peace, and form spaces of democracy.[77] PAR is thus distinguishable from other forms of research by its action component and by being carried out on a group basis (rather than by external researchers independently). It involves praxis, or reflecting on what needs to be done, taking action, and reflecting on that action.

Susan Smith proposes that "a holistic framework for PAR methodology must capture dynamic, lived experience, or '*vivencia*,' acknowledging people as complex beings with different motivations, perceptions, capabilities, feelings and relationships, but with shared problems and desires for community and common effort. It must make room for the necessary dialectical tensions and conflicts."[78]

PAR has been critiqued by postcolonial, feminist, and critical international development scholars for its origins in Western development paradigms, its potential perpetuation of colonial relations, and its frequent implementation in projects led by outsiders.[79] At the same time, however, Indigenous researchers have found resonance in its relational epistemology and emancipatory methodology.[80] Feminists have brought a gender lens to critiques of PAR, challenging the composition of research teams, the issues researched, and the emerging analyses.[81] Such critical questioning did not escape VIVA! partners as we reflected on our local and transnational processes:

in the video of Tianguis Cultural, for example, women question the lack of female leadership in the organization; in our own annual gatherings, we noted that the major organizing was handled by women partners, even when the country hosts were male. Race and gender (and class) converged in the dynamic of the domination by white women in community arts projects in the North.

On the other hand, there are several ways in which the VIVA! process has been informed by certain feminist epistemological questions and methodological practices:

- Adopting an intersecting analysis of power;

- Honoring local and historically contingent practices but within a context of globalizing processes;

- Focusing on situated knowledges and collaborative knowledge production;

- Promoting self-reflexivity about the internal power dynamics of the project;

- Using arts-based research methods to examine arts-based educational practices, that challenge body/mind and reason/emotion dichotomies;

- Developing an ecological and feminist analysis of interconnectedness toward a more holistic popular education;

- Countering top-down imposition of structures and processes, remaining open to emergent and unexpected questions and insights;

- Advocating praxis both in a theory/practice dialectic of research and in a commitment to political action emerging from the community arts and popular education processes.[82]

PAR has also been a fertile ground for the development of arts-based research methods, a growing field within education, health, and social science research. The Center for Arts-Informed Research at the University of Toronto has published numerous volumes in the past decade, focusing on a wide range of arts-based methods in qualitative research,[83] on multimedia methods,[84] on visual inquiry,[85] and dissertations in alternative forms,[86] among others. Ardra Cole and Gary Knowles, codirec-

tors of the center, suggest that "the central purpose of arts-informed research is to enhance understanding of the human condition through alternative (to conventional) processes and representational forms of inquiry, and to reach multiple audiences by making scholarship more accessible."[87]

In contrast to "arts-informed research," Susan Finley distinguishes "arts-based research," locating it in the realm of socially transformative approaches:

By its integration of multiple methodologies used in the arts with the postmodern ethics of participative, action-oriented, and politically situated perspectives for human social inquiry, arts-based inquiry has the potential to facilitate critical race, Indigenous, queer, feminist and border theories and research methodologies. As a form of performance pedagogy, arts-based inquiry can be used to advance a subversive political agenda that addresses issues of social inequity.[88]

One of the complexities of the VIVA! project is that both the content and the process of the research have been art based; thus we are using art as a method to reflect on community arts practices. Our approach draws from the rich understandings of the power of the arts in learning as well as the suggestion that it can empower social action, as suggested earlier.

While PAR offered a common language and practice for both Spanish-speaking Latin American and English-speaking North American collaborators in VIVA!, the Latin partners suggested that their related practice of *sistematización* was perhaps more suited to their purposes when outside facilitators are not needed, as it engages participants in a program or project in a focused reflection on their shared experience for the purpose of understanding it more deeply, potentially impacting their subsequent actions.[89] We adapted *sistematización* as a process for deepening our collective analysis of projects during our annual meetings.

Nor were these processes without their contradictions, however; Laura Reinsborough, a VIVA! intern working with our Panamanian partner, was asked to facilitate a process of *sistematización* with the Kuna Children's Art Workshop participants, and grappled with the contradictions of taking on such a role as an outsider to the context, project, and process.[90] While understanding her contribution as a documenter, Laura reflected on the limitations:

> the most important rule of *sistematización* is that only those who have participated in the experience are able to evaluate and reflect upon it. Therefore, the stories of the participants comprise the central elements for analysis and reflection. The process is also collaborative, as it engages the participants in all levels of the research: from gathering people's experiences to sharing their reflections, and from designing the research plan to evaluating and analysing the findings. The role of documentation is emphasized, not just for an archive but also for a deepening of critical reflection. In addition, *sistematización* is considered "self-research," meaning that it asserts that the responsibility of theorizing from the lived experiences rests with the participants, not with an outside institution.[91]

The application of PAR and *sistematización* in the local projects varied, and there were perhaps certain moments when the contradictions were most acute: for example, the writing of the chapters for this book, which in some cases was highly collaborative, and in other cases not. The video documentation, too, is shaped by one videographer or director's perspective on a project. We understand that any and all of these efforts reflect partial knowledge (adopting a poststructural stance) but at the same time, we hope that they will generate critical reflection by the readers, not only of these cases, but also of their own practice. Ultimately, we combine transformative methodologies (more influenced by Eurocentric critical social thought) with both non-Western and poststructural methodologies. This messy and unfinished dialogue, in fact, has provided some of the richest parts of our transnational exchange, and needs to continue.

Firm grounding

This chapter has introduced the theoretical and methodological foundations of the VIVA! project: decolonization, popular education, community arts, and participatory action research. When these interrelated practices are firmly rooted and offer a strong base for community-engaged processes, they hopefully birth creative processes of knowledge production and inspire individuals and groups to express themselves and to act collectively to challenge inequities and to create more sustainable and just communities, ecologies, and nations as well as a shared planet. The chapters that follow bring these practices alive in their very particular historical and geopolitical contexts and in all their complexity. And through the diverse voices of the VIVA! partners.

See Paulo Freire, *Pedagogy of the Oppressed* (New York: Herder and Herder, 1970), 60.

PART I

Recovering Cultural Histories

Engaging Creative Tensions in Indigenous and Diasporic Contexts

INTRODUCTION

This section features two projects that are responses to the devastating impact of colonialism, slavery, and forced migration on Indigenous and African and other racialized people in the Americas—the Kuna Children's Art Workshops in Panama and the Personal Legacy project in Canada. But before delving into these specific practices, I introduce one of the first frameworks we collectively developed as a transnational team for analyzing our work.

At our first transnational gathering of VIVA! partners in 2003, we crafted the notion of "creative tensions" as a way of looking dialectically at our community arts and popular education practices. We did not want to take either a purely celebratory approach nor a defensive one; rather we wanted to acknowledge the messiness and challenges of this counter-hegemonic work, and adopt a self-critical stance. We started with five key tensions: process/product, aesthetics/ethics, cultural reclamation / cultural reinvention, spiritual/political, and body/earth. In delineating them, I draw from the rich experience and dialogue of VIVA! partners—expressed in our transnational gatherings as well as in the chapters to come.

Process/product

> Cultural promotion is a journey. The greatest strength of the Tianguis Cultural (or cultural marketplace) is the city's young people, who claim their space in society and will fight for it.[1]
> —Leonardo David de Anda Gonzalez and Sergio Eduardo Martínez
> Mayoral, Guadalajara, Mexico

Popular education and community art both foreground the *processes* of collective knowledge production and art-making, in contrast with the banking education that Brazilian educator Paulo Freire so eloquently challenged, and the elitist, individualized, and commodified art promoted

Collective mural production at York University

by Western thought and its extension, corporate globalization. This does not deny the importance of an end product, which may then generate other processes when shared in community.

This tension was explored in several VIVA! projects. Toronto's Catalyst Centre trained young artists in the Telling Our Stories project to facilitate community art-making with youth, breaking out of the dominant mode of their individual artistic productions to lead processes that help young people develop self-confidence, break silences, and build community. Nonetheless, a culminating event in Toronto's Lula Lounge provided the impetus to finish some products—and perform them—from break dancing to spoken word.

Christine McKenzie describes how this was a new insight for one young artist, who had focused on creating spectacles, or performances, without taking into account how the audience could get involved:

> Doing something that's a spectacle doesn't always make people critically engaged, bring people together, or challenge barriers between people.

That's one thing he took from the workshop, so his next project included youth taking questions into neighborhoods, learning from each other.

Even though the young artists in the Telling Our Stories project didn't call themselves "community artists," Christine continues,

> they grabbed on to the idea of critical issues coming out through art. And they changed their ideas about how to do the art, like digging up historical roots of the music or dance they're performing, so people can learn about where it came from and how they're related to that, rather than just doing break dancing.

The process thus took on a new importance for them. They were excited, too, to see how the youth responded; in a Hip Cuban Hop project, two artist/animators reported that the girls seemed to take pride in doing something healthy (physically and mentally), positive and empowering.

Faye Dupras, director of "Bridge of One Hair" with Joy Douglas and Wanda Krane

Aesthetics/ethics

Art always involves striving towards a vision, and generally falling short. But this does not change the fact that aesthetics and ethics are best friends. It is through being artists to the best of our abilities, with all the complexity, expansiveness and unexpectedness of artistic solutions, that we can serve, respond to and express the communities with which we engage. To go further: through not striving fully on an aesthetic level we place ourselves in an unethical position in relation to these communities from whom we are asking so much.

—Ruth Howard, Jumblies Theatre, Toronto

Issues of aesthetics and ethics are central to community arts practice, and we have had rich debates within the VIVA! project about our different approaches to this tension. Canadian theater artist Ruth Howard insists that it is the art-making that drives the work; collaborating artist Faye Dupras further develops this position in the Jumblies video:

In community-based art, we as artists need to be engaged and stimulated in creating art that is worthy and that we're excited about. It's not OK to look at it and say, "Oh, that's not great, but hey, the community was engaged." It's not because aesthetics are important, it's because my passion, my spirit needs to be awakened and the community's spirit needs to be awakened, and then there's a real meeting point.

Mexican graphic artist Sergio G. (Checo) Valdez has taken quite a different position in the community-based mural production process, Pintar Obedeciendo, or Painting by Listening. Whether working closely with street youth in Mexico City or with Zapatista autonomous communities in Chiapas to create murals celebrating their own histories, Valdez refuses to impose any of his own ideas or aesthetic values.

Valdez contrasts community arts with more dominant practices. He looks back on four decades of his work as an illustrator, and considers the ego of the artist an obstacle in community arts: "When we make participatory community murals, we have to renounce our ego, contain our ego; it's a spiritual exercise." He sees this approach as similar to the historical understanding of artisan work: The artisan constructs, adapts traditions, is meticulous and anonymous. He doesn't work from his ego.

The distinguishing feature of community arts, for Checo, is that both the content and the process are determined by the community. Valdez distinguishes his approach as being *from* the community, while other approaches to community mural production work *with* or make representations *of* the community, with the artist still playing a major role in terms of aesthetics. Checo's experience with Indigenous communities in Chiapas, Mexico, challenged dominant art practices through productions that turned the people themselves into artists and their own local heroes into the subject of their art:

> This represented a significant shift. In Chiapas there are nine hundred painted walls. Of these, there may be as many as fifteen, and I may be exaggerating because it could be less, fifteen murals painted by Indigenous people. The great majority have been produced by people who come from the outside with their own vision of the Indigenous people and their social movements in the region. They come, they sign their work and they leave, and many times don't even stay long enough to get to know the people. So we decided it was better to listen to them, to see how they paint. We let them construct their own reality. We help them if we can, mainly by encouraging these gatherings and discussions.

Cultural reclamation / cultural reinvention

As community art is often identified with marginalized groups and communities, with people whose histories have been hidden or discredited, processes of participatory research and collective art-making involve what Central American popular educators call *recuperación histórica-cultural* or cultural reclamation. Maori educator Linda Tuhiwai Smith suggests that "coming to know the past" is central to a process of decolonization, especially for communities whose ways of knowing have been driven underground or destroyed by institutions, such as the residential schools in Canada.[2] For Indigenous communities like the Kuna Yala in Panama, art is a tool in this process of reclamation; the Kuna Children's Art Workshops used storytelling, drawing, mask-making, theater, song, and dance to recover Kuna cultural stories and values. But such recovery projects do not unearth a culture frozen in time; cultures are internally complex and their members' ways of expressing themselves are constantly changing, being recreated.

VIVA! partner José Angel Colman recalls the challenge of becoming a Kuna artist in Panama in the 1970s:

> When I went to university, I wanted to study theatre and they asked me why; I hid the fact that I also danced, because it was considered strange. They didn't accept me in the theatre program. One professor told me: "You have to make your own theatre, for you there is no script."

Diane Roberts had a similar experience as the only black performance student in a Canadian university theater course, where she felt pressured to conform to classic forms and to believe there was a universal aesthetic. José Angel struggled with dual influences:

> We were being formed in our own traditions as Indigenous people to be able to project ourselves outward because we learned western thought by force and by obligation through colonization. From our birth on, the Christian church was there teaching us the Bible, one plus one, the ABCs of another culture. Thanks to my grandfather I was taught traditional ways before I went to school. But for many years I was lost in my community. I spoke Spanish! But it's also very rich that I can now interact with people from other parts of the world and manage other cultures. And today the

Mural entitled "Dove of Land and Liberty," Cerro Hueco Prison, Chiapas, 1998

Young anarchist activist sells symbols in the marketplace

project deepens our understanding of what it means to recover one's ancestral history, embedded in our bodies; Diane Roberts calls it a process of reclamation, a process of resistance and a process of transformation. Jumblies Theatre's Bridge of One Hair project is about bringing diverse communities together as they reinvent themselves in their adopted countries, both respecting distinct practices as well as creating new fusions of cultural forms. BilwiVision, the community television station on the Caribbean Coast of Nicaragua, aims to create space on the airwaves for Miskitu, Creole, and mestizo peoples who are crafting their own coexistence in the context of autonomy from the national government. The cultural marketplace in Guadalajara, Tianguis Cultural, is also about the convergence of youth with very different identities, who are linking their right to self-expression with those of the Huichol people, for example, aiming to create a more tolerant urban culture as well as alliances for social struggles.

Kuna Congress is recognized and we have our own school. The churches are now regulated by the Congress, they can preach but can't criticize the Kuna religion; in fact, they've adjusted their schedules to the Kuna traditional time.

José continues,

I think this was the importance of the Kuna Children's Art Workshops because they were flexible in spirit and accepting of others. The workshops in the late 1990s have also inspired a potential new project with the children, who lived on the islands when they participated in the art workshops. Now they are adolescents living in Panama City and reinventing themselves in a new urban multicultural context.

Many of the VIVA! projects described in this book combine a process of recovering traditional history and culture, with the collective creation of new cultures, based on multiple and distinct identities. The Personal Legacy

*Indigenous jewelry maker at work in
Tianguis Cultural, Guadalajara, Mexico*

Jesús Alemancia sharing a Kuna story at the Harvesting Stories conference

Spiritual/political

The secular has been divested of the sacred and the spiritual of the political.
    —M. Jacqui Alexander, *Pedagogies of Crossing:*
    Meditations on Feminism, Sexual Politics,
    Memory and the Sacred

The powerful voices of a growing number of diasporic and Indigenous activists and artists challenge the spiritual/political dichotomy in the thought and practice of Western activists and ideologues. For Linda Tuhiwai Smith, Indigenous spiritualities, which Christianity tried to destroy, are critical sites of resistance, "one of the few parts of ourselves which the West cannot decipher, cannot understand, and cannot control . . . yet."[3]

Participants in the Personal Legacy project are exploring how their processes of reclaiming ancestral memory in their bodies, both a personal and political

process, is also "a spiritual journey," as Heather Hermant suggests. Diane Roberts emphasizes that it is artistic work and "we are not engaging in ceremonial or shamanic practice." As the process is evolving, however, she muses:

There are some spiritual aspects to the work that we've sort of stumbled onto (or into). Now having said that, it would be inaccurate to say that we "stumbled" upon these aspects, since my attempt to work within an African aesthetic where spiritual practice and arts practice are often intertwined is so central to the process.

In fact, it is the Western tendency to separate spirituality from politics, from education and organizing, that the VIVA! project challenges. This has been a particularly difficult shift for political activists informed by Marxist thought, who denounced religion as the "opiate of the masses"; there has been a false conflation of institutionalized religion and spirituality. Yet, especially in diasporic contexts, community arts can provide spaces for the recognition and contribution of various spiritualities; the ritual dimensions of community art-making processes themselves are often imbued with a spiritual dimension. All aspects of a person are honored in creative processes that tap hearts, minds, and spirits.

VIVA! project collaborators have both created rituals and explored them in our annual gatherings; the Harvesting Stories conference in Toronto in late October 2004 culminated in a cultural evening, Beyond Halloween: Celebrating Life and Death, allowing us to share stories from Anishnabe and Kuna, Mexican and European traditions that honor the dead, and reveal, in fact, very distinct worldviews of the processes of living and dying. Our storytelling was followed the next evening by a community event in Toronto, Night of Dread, which has appropriated the Day of the Dead to involve a downtown neighborhood in parading their fears with large puppets and masks. At our 2006 gathering in Chiapas, Mexico, pairs of participants created opening rituals that drew upon particular traditions and created new ones. Often they were linked to an understanding of the spirit in all living things of the natural world.

Body/earth

> At the center of this (Personal Legacy) process is the acknowledgment that everything we need to draw on for inspiration is stored in our bodies as memory.
> —Diane Roberts, Canada

Contrasting notions of life and death expressed in stories during the Beyond Halloween event actually reveal another deep Western dualism, the separation of human and nonhuman nature, body and earth. The Mohawk people in Ontario describe their world as "All Our Relations," and thank all elements, plants and animals as well as human kin, in their prayers. Mohawk writer Beth Brant emphasizes this equality quite simply: "We do not worship nature. We are part of it."[4]

Also invoking Indigenous cosmovisions, Central American popular educators have developed the concept of *integralidad*, or holism, to emphasize a pedagogical practice that embraces embodied and analytical knowing, theory, and practice, and affirms the interconnectedness of all living entities. The Panamanian hosts of our second international team meeting in August 2005 deliberately located the five-day gathering in an ecological center in the midst of the jungle, where we could be daily reminded through the sounds, smells, heat, and humidity that we are part of a vibrant biocentric community. Some of the local projects uncover the impact of human blindness to that connection. Jumblies Theatre, for example, always researches the ecological history of the Toronto neighborhoods where they work.

In the Panamanian context, José Angel Colman reveals some of the ways Indigenous people were colonized through control of their bodies as well as their lands.

> Some Kunas prohibited dancing, because they were influenced by the church, which tried to sanitize everything as they Christianized us. In certain communities, people believed that dancing would wake up the spirits and that people would get sick. But through the Kuna Children's Art Workshops, they saw children from other islands dancing, and now there are dance groups in those places; they even tour outside the community.

The denial of the body encouraged by Christianity was further racialized and sexualized in Eurocentric stereotypes of women of color, for example the Creole and Miskitu women on the Caribbean Coast of Nicaragua. VIVA! partner Margarita Antonio denounces this stigma of coastal women as loose and hot, and encourages the young team working at their community television station, BilwiVision, to challenge these representations:

> On the coast, we say that we only appear in the national media when there are earthquakes, floods, drugs, or women dancing. In our community channel, we have to be careful not to reproduce these stereotypes, we have to decolonize ourselves.

Diane Roberts, whose Personal Legacy project, is based in a reclamation of the body as a source of memory and knowledge, offers another interpretation of the images of Nicaraguan women dancing:

Kuna dancers at the Carti Sugdup Community Centre, Panama City

I didn't see the women dancing as an exotic piece, I didn't look at the hips moving in a sexualized way, but I was rather interested in the relation of the dancers to the drums . . . and the communication that was going back and forth . . . to be able to use what was actually happening and build on that, and create spaces where the dialogue can actually happen.

The Personal Legacy work is in itself a challenge to the colonized body. As Diane contextualizes it:

There is an ancestral war dance between the colonizer and the colonized, between the slave master and the slave, between the European explorer and the African warrior. The battle manifests itself daily, in my mind, my hips, my knees, my feet, my ankles, my joints, my blood, my bones, my tongue . . . my being.

The process moves us toward a deeper understanding of our selves as part of nature, but shaped by brutal colonial histories, such as the slave trade, that are inscribed on bodies as well as on the land: "This river of blood I refer to fed the land, makes the land grow, and mixes with the blood of all the ancestors in this room."

Amy Shimshon-Santo sees the ArtsBridge program in Los Angeles as an entry point for young students in inner-city schools, many of whom share a colonial history and who have become disconnected from both their homelands and their ancestral identities:

> Dance education is a powerful forum for analyzing the Body/Earth tension. Movement education challenges many deeply seated stereotypes about knowledge, the body, and identity. The legacy of Cartesian thinking undergirds many scholastic programs and continues to downplay the importance of body knowledge.

Embodied knowing and learning, in fact, has become a key theme for the VIVA! project and is reflected in several project chapters.

Two projects challenging colonized lands, bodies, and minds

The following two chapters embody many of these creative tensions and have been heavily referenced in this introduction. While Jesús Alemancia focuses on the recovery of Kuna cultural values among children in Kuna Yala in the 1990s, he also concludes in the present with the challenge of engaging these children, now young adults living as internal migrants in cosmopolitan Panama City. Similarly, Diane Roberts's Personal Legacy project, which began as a process of recovering ancestral memory, has evolved into The Arrivals project, involving emerging artists in Indigenous and diasporic communities across Canada in understanding more deeply not only their hidden histories but also "their present self, family and community."

Both projects also counter the impact of dominant formal education processes that have suppressed or denied culturally specific and embodied ways of knowing: the Kuna Children's Art Workshops were responses to a gap in public education classes taught by mestizos with little knowledge of Kuna culture, and ultimately created a tension between the nonformal workshops and school classes, where attendance began to drop. Diane Roberts

initiated the Personal Legacy project in response to her own Western theater training that forced her Afro-Caribbean body into Eurocentric movements and practices. Both projects, then, attempted to liberate the "colonized body" in uncovering deep body memories and in returning precolonial dance traditions, for example, to their central role in community celebrations.

CHAPTER 1

PLANTING GOOD SEEDS

The Kuna Children's Art Workshops

Jesús Alemancia, CEASPA, Kuna Yala, Panama

I come home to you very poor, mother,
I picked up my bundle of sweaty clothes
and saw that there was nothing left in the gourd
of the fresh *chicha*[1]
that I, your teenager, took away some moons ago.

Here I am, mother,
your small hunter herding spears
feeling unloved and frightened,
with a poor person's hammock roughly rolled up.
I come to you hurting, mother,
I have suckled the breasts of Kueloyai
and among so many foreign influences
I even lost my name
and you know that's not how to fight:

I am like a boy waking up
without his little kayak . . .

Mother, I drag myself home,
wearing this tie, I come to you hurting,
wearing these fashionable moccasins,
I come to you hurting,
with this raised body, I am bleeding,
with this new face, I am bleeding. . . .

Mother, whisper words of forgiveness,
civilize my heart once again,
and make of it a barricade
because now I must stay at home . . .

—Aiban Wagua,
"Civiliza Mi Corazón, Mamá," *La Tinaja Kuna*

As a Kuna and the director of CEASPA, the Panamanian Social Education and Action Center, I recall the Kuna Children's Art Workshops as an important example of the integration of arts into popular and environmental education. CEASPA helped train the project facilitators in popular education methods. We chose to systematize or reflect upon this project as part of the VIVA! exchange, because it was about the recovery of our history and culture in the deepest sense. This process of reflecting has been a collaborative one, involving facilitators in the project as well as a VIVA! intern.[2]

The beginnings

In 1993, a group of youth from the Duiren Sapingan organization in the Kuna Yala region of Panama, together

Dock at Carti Sugdup Island, Kuna Yala

with the Education Office of the Smithsonian Tropical Research Institute (STRI), initiated a process of environmental education in various Kuna Yala communities, guided by the concepts and methodologies of popular education with the participation of primary school children, as well as youth who were not part of the formal school system.

What led to this educational endeavor was some research on hunting and subsistence within the Kuna community.[3] The researcher had promised the community authorities that he would return what he learned to the community. He fulfilled this commitment by producing a coloring book for children called *Anmar Napguana Minmigana*, or *We, the Children of Mother Earth*, in 1989. Later, as the children's coloring book began to circulate in Kuna Yala primary schools, two additional blank pages were included so that the Kuna children could send their drawings on their environmental surroundings to a contest by STRI and the Regional Board of Directors of Education of Kuna Yala.

Jorge Ventocilla, the researcher, describes the origins and beginning of this creative adventure:

What did we do to fulfill what we had offered? We put together all the information we had about fifteen animals and the Kuna in a coloring book that talks about animals, what they eat and where they live. We included some sheets so that the children could make their own drawings and texts, and invited them to participate in an art contest. When we got these drawings, around 1990, they were so beautiful and the children's texts so magnificent, that it was logical to think, why don't we create or facilitate a space where the Kuna children could develop, express and exhibit the great creativity they had. That was the idea for the children's art workshops.[4]

As a result of the drawing contest the idea to implement a Kuna Children's Art Workshop was born in Ailigandi, one of the Kuna Yala communities. Afterward, in this same community, the first gathering of Kuna artists was organized. From these experiences the network of Kuna Children's Art Workshops came to be, a process that developed between 1993 and 2000.

Children's drawing

Kuna band at festival

Ventocilla emphasizes that from the beginning, the project organizers agreed that "the artists are essential, essential in the sense that they embody the essence of their peoples, whether they are Indigenous or not; they maintain the culture, they recreate it, they express it. Recognizing this, we also wanted to nurture artistic development. We wanted to participate in this process."

The richness of this process was the combination of two educational approaches, environmental education and popular education. Both approaches were woven together with the Kuna cultural context and pedagogical use of art—painting, theater, dance, music, song, poetry. It was an innovative process that could be easily reproduced in other communities, that opened up new educational paths.

For CEASPA, the experience confirmed that our processes of accompanying and supporting Indigenous community organizations had tangible results, since those who facilitated the Kuna Children's Art Workshops networks were trained as leaders and popular educators in our methodological schools of popular education. This is how one of the participants, José Angel Colman, remembers it:

> We were part of CEASPA. There were field trips, tours, rich moments of exchange. The methodological schools helped us become aware of the current social situation. For example, the monthly seminars of conjunctural analysis, sessions in which not only did we talk about Indigenous issues, but also national and international developments.

Jorge Ventocilla and Kuna poet Arysteides Turpana in children's art workshop

31

In this process of popular education we do not see ourselves being formed or trained as Indigenous, as Indigenous to be Indigenous, to be contained within that. We are forming ourselves in our own traditional schools as Indigenous in order to be able to project ourselves outward because we already have the knowledge of Western culture by force and by obligation.

The broader context

Panama is one of the most unique countries in Latin America. Geographically, it is part of Central America; it is the southern border of the region. Historically, however, it does not have much of a relationship with Central America; it was a department (province) of Colombia until 1903, so it was part of the history of South America and a Bolivarian country.[5] Culturally, it is a multicultural country; in such a small territory (75,517 km²), its population has a great cultural diversity.

One of the most representative cultural communities of this great cultural diversity are the Indigenous peoples (10 percent of the national population of almost three million inhabitants, according to the 2000 census). There are seven Indigenous communities: the Ngöbe; Buglé; Naso; Bri-bri in the western part of the country; and in the east, the Kuna, Emberá, and Wounaa. The majority of this population lives in the tropical forests of the country, which in some cases are protected by environmental laws; they are considered *comarcas* or regional territories that are legally recognized by the Panamanian state.

One of 365 islands in the Kuna Yala archipelago

Alemancia family, Carti Sugdup

Kuna Yala is one of these *comarcal* territories, located in northeastern Panama, covering an area of 3,206 km[2]. It is divided into two regions, one made up of mainland territory and the other made up of islands. The mainland includes both a mountainous area and a coastal zone. The mountainous area is covered with old-growth forests and reaches an altitude of 400–1350 meters. The coastal zone is characterized by a complex pattern of old-growth forests in some areas, secondary forests in all of the successive stages, and small plantations along the rivers and the coast, where coconut trees abound. Mangroves, palms trees, and fruit trees are the most common vegetation in the coastal area. The island region includes more than 360 small coralline islands all along the coast.

In 1990, the Kuna Yala population was 34,044 inhabitants; by 2000 there were only 32,446 inhabitants (15,154 men and 17,292 women) who were on the islands.[6] Kuna communities are organized around the *Onmaked Nega* or communal assembly, presided over by a *Saila*, a political and religious community leader. The community assembly is the maximum authority, known as the Local Congress; this is where decisions of social, political, economic, and religious character are discussed and made. In daily deliberations and discussions of the Local Congresses, any member of the communities is heard by the *Saila*, who ultimately makes decisions based on a consensus of the assembly. Issues that concern and impact the *comarcal* territory are debated in the *Onmaked Dummad Sunmakaled* or General Congress, the assembly of all of the Kuna Yala communities. Three *Saila Dunmagen* preside over the General Congress, and as spokespersons, they communicate decisions made in the Kuna general assembly to the Panamanian government.

Other community leaders of the Local Congress are the *Argargan Suaribgan*[7] and *Sapin Dummagan*.[8] In terms of art, the *Argargan* are an important support to the *Saila* as they sing and interpret the symbology of the traditional songs that the *Saila* performs (because the traditional songs were performed in metaphoric language, they need to be translated into ordinary language).

The social structure of the Kuna community is sustained by the family unit, which is matrilocal, so the male spouse is integrated into the home of his in-laws; women

Carti Sugdup Community Center, Panama City, 2006

The Kuna Yala region currently faces an accelerated destruction, loss of biodiversity and of traditional knowledge. There are tremendous external pressures on Indigenous communities and their original cultures to integrate into the national dominant culture through economic, social, educational, and cultural policies that are insensitive to the Kuna culture. These policies affect the traditional Kuna social structure and thus threaten the survival of Indigenous cultures and the maintenance and reproduction of their traditional knowledge and practices. They impose foreign values that attack and destroy traditional values of local culture, provoking a chain reaction of rapid changes with sociocultural and environmental consequences that are difficult to manage. The loss of this cultural knowledge also accompanies an accelerated erosion of the biodiversity in the region. Teonila Herrera, one of the Kuna artists, reflects on this loss:

> Most people in my community no longer prac-
> tice their culture. We no longer use the *mola*.
> We no longer make baskets or fans. Because our
> elders have died, and they did not pass on this
> heritage to us.

The project

After the first gathering of Kuna artists in Ailigandi in 1993, the Kuna Children's Art Workshops network was formally established in 1995. It was supported by the Canadian embassy and initially involved the communities of Mandi Yala, Ukupseni, Akuanusadup, and Carti Sugdup.
The objectives of the project were:

- To give importance to Kuna children, so that within and outside of the *Comarca* (region) adults would pay more attention to the children, to their life circumstances and to their potential;

- To promote the children's knowledge of their own cultural values, understanding culture as ranging from artistic expressions to the principles of human solidarity;

- To instill in children knowledge that allows them to better appreciate their ecological environment, so that eventually they would participate in their society, reclaiming a just use of nature.

are highly valued in Kuna culture. They still maintain their traditional styles of clothing: *la mola* or blouses with designs that represent nature, skirts of one fabric, and a handkerchief. Women's traditional attire is completed by jewellery on their legs, hands, ears, and nose as well as facial designs. The men no longer wear their traditional clothes except on special occasions. Even though the rituals are slowly disappearing, some forms of traditional healing are still practiced, among them, the celebration of puberty, the traditional wedding, and dances.

The methodology

One main strategy to accomplish these objectives was the Kuna children's art festivals. These festivals were made up of three components: environmental education, popular education, and art. The methodology of the project was based on these three approaches, aimed at developing an experience in environmental education among Kuna children that was both within and outside of the formal education system, and instilling within them a spirit of concern for and conservation of the environment. It was a particular challenge to have the children of a specific Indigenous culture like the Kuna as a target group for environmental education.

The latent potential of play and creativity in the children, the cultural richness of the Kuna cosmology, and the way that the *molas* were designed (later reflected in the visual arts) were all present in the process. The challenge was how to make all this a dynamic force for *recuperación* or recovery and promotion of cultural identity within the framework of an environmental education process. This challenge was met by implementing three central components of the work:

- The art workshops offered spaces for training and creativity among the children and youth of the communities. The workshop themes reflected life in the communities and activities aimed at developing artistic skills in theater, painting, dances, songs, recitation, and music. These workshops were ongoing in each participating community.

- Another component was the children's art festivals, celebrated once a year with all of the children, coinciding with the anniversary of the Tule Revolution[9] in February. People from the communities, local authorities, facilitators, the children, and educators participated, as well as non-Kuna artists who offered their experiences and creativity as poets, musicians, and photographers. The festivals were a great display of artistic creativity and an opportunity for dialogue among youth, children, and elders about the people's culture and future.

- The third component of the program was the *formación* or training of the *promotores*, or facilitators. The

Poster for festival of Kuna art

facilitators received training in popular education with an emphasis on participatory methodologies. They also developed cultural knowledge and the artistic skills necessary for the facilitation of the art workshops and the organization of the festivals, as well as aspects related to the environment. The training included sociocultural facilitation, group work methodology, workshop organization, and specific artistic skills selected for the work with children.

Other program elements contributed to the building of a network of workshops. For example, children who did not attend primary school received informal classes in reading and writing in the community of Ukupseny taught

by international interns who supported the art workshops network. There were field trips organized outside of Kuna Yala, to Panama City, as a reward for facilitators as well as for children who won art contests in the festival. During these trips they got to know the city and visited biological research centers as well as areas where the migrant Kuna population lived.

Lessons and limitations of the project

The Kuna Children's Art Workshop experience was pioneering and successful in the field of environmental education and cultural promotion. The project's contributions were various. From the perspective of environmental education, this initiative connected socioenvironmental research processes to environmental education with Indigenous children. In practice, it affirmed the value of Kuna cosmology and, in particular, the Kuna vision of nature, which served as the foundation for this educational experience. Another important element was how the environmental project applied popular education methodologies that involved youth from the communities, children both inside and outside of the primary school system of Kuna Yala, educational authorities, Kuna spiritual leaders, and the community in general. The participation of this diversity of actors was fostered by incorporating the daily relationship between culture and nature, an important element for environmental pedagogy and teaching. Kuna artist Ologuagdi Díaz describes this relationship:

> We, the community, the Kuna nation, developed our consciousness through a popular education process that has to do with life itself. When we talk about life itself, we are talking about the Earth, Mother Earth, the grandmother, the sea, the tree, our sister tree. What does this mean? These are resources we have to be able to work with to make something that is beautiful, that is art. It is in this way that we are making art, just like the sand which was once stone, then, is changed by force of the water. We created games so that the children could feel the sea, the sand; I used this playful approach to learning about nature because it interested me. . . . The Western world may call it H_2O, but for us it's a sister, our Sister Water.

The process was stimulating from the perspective of Kuna identity. We started from the principles of education expressed by the Kuna leadership, teaching the children the values of Kuna culture. Many children who are part of the official educational system—from prekindergarten to grade 3—are in the hands of Latino educators who educate them in the values of Western culture. Children who were not part of the formal educational system were also incorporated into this space where they could develop artistic skills within their cultural context.

The workshops were based on the *recuperación* or recovery of all of the arts used by the ancestors and maintained by the elders in the community to feed back to the community their artistic expressions—songs, dances, poetry, oral narrations, paintings, and music. The project also recovered cultural understandings of nature based on the historical experiences of the Kuna people and their vision of marine and mainland nature as creators of life. This was complemented with visits to different natural sites in the *comarca* where these children learned Indigenous knowledge through experiential education.

The Kuna Children's Art Workshops also promoted the recovery of Kuna dances in the community of Carti Sugdup where they were no longer practiced. The art workshops organized a children's dance group there. Kuna songs and music had a great impact in a musical production, which had the children as central participants. This production was performed outside of Kuna Yala, nationally and even internationally. One of the cultural facilitators, Teonila Herrera, describes the impact that the workshops had on the children:

> We talked about culture. We talked about *our* culture. We talked about Diegun, about Ibeler (characters from the oral Kuna tradition), because the children did not know anything of these histories. They learned a lot of these things. In our community this workshop was very important. Sometimes the children would ask when the workshop was going to begin. It seemed like they liked it.

From the perspective of popular education there were also important contributions. The methodology was effective, participatory and motivational in the work with children. A basic lesson was that in order for the project to get started, it was important that it be accepted by members

Environmental field trip, Kuna Children's Art Workshops

of the Kuna community, in particular the local authorities. It was necessary to involve not only the children but also all the members of the communities. With the support of the community and its leaders, it was possible throughout the project to involve the elders, who are the holders of the Kuna wisdom, in discussions and reflections with cultural facilitators and project participants. They were the teachers of the cultural formation of the children and workshop participants.

The youth facilitators developed and deepened their leadership potential throughout the process of the art workshops. They were active participants in the community organizational processes, eventually taking on positions like the town secretary, a very important responsibility within Kuna communities. Sociocultural facilitation was a critical component of the workshops, applying innovative methodologies such as incorporating Kuna stories and promoting dialogue among the youth, children, and elders of the communities.

The participation of children who were not part of the formal education system generated some critical reflection among members of the art workshops. In one of the communities, Ukupseni, for example, there was a gathering with children who did not have the opportunity to go to school. These children had no other space where they could benefit from nonformal education. The workshops gave them an opportunity to develop their creativity and to consolidate their cultural identity.

Kuna children on Carti Sugdup island

The process of popular education through art nurtured the development of the children's self-esteem and cultural identity. As Evelio López, one of the workshop coordinators, emphasizes:

> Art is important so that children can learn, develop their self-esteem, and create their own imagination. Art is important not only for the children, but also for the community. Through theater, music, poetry, the community can also learn and contribute.
>
> Kuna culture is full of poetry, so art is an important medium. We need to support culture, to strengthen our identity; through different media we can generate cultural themes and create expressions of identity. The workshops were open, so any boy or girl could choose a theme; they had a lot of freedom to participate, to express their creativity. The workshop offered this space for the children to do their own art-making.

The high point was when the communities and the children were excited about making their own theater, writing their own poetry. This process raised their self-esteem both as children and as Indigenous people.

As with any educational process, the results of our efforts were revealed over time. The impact was only felt bit by bit, some time after the workshops had finished. José Angel Colman, one of the artist facilitators, tells this story:

> In working with people, with children, in the moment, many times people expect results; they want to see something concrete and immediate. But working with human beings is much more than just results, it is a *formación*, or development process. It's motivating, it generates interest in the children, but you don't see results from one day to the next; there's a process of maturing. Because you are beginning to work with ideas, to build ex-

periences in the children's minds and this process is very important.

Ten years pass and you begin to see results when you are no longer thinking about it. For example, the children who were eight or ten years old at the time of the project, now are twenty years old and some are in university. . . . One youth moved from his community to the city of Chitre. It appears that after many years passed, this young man always kept in mind that experience of the children's art workshops.

We had lost contact with this him, but he found us. He sent us an email, telling us that he wanted to become a writer. That he wanted his first experience as a writer to focus on his grandmother's life and life in his community. That is why he was studying journalism. We planted something in that boy who is now a young man. You can see his interest in continuing to explore the ideas from this experience in his childhood.

Limitations

The Kuna Children's Art Workshops continued until 2000, and only ended then for two reasons. First, the decision was to keep the project organization (funds, decisions, and so forth) centralized in Panama City and not to transfer it to the workshops themselves in the *Comarcas*. Second, in 1999, the responsibility of the entire project was handed over to the Duiren organization, something we had planned from the start. But then Duiren entered into a crisis period and could not give the project the ongoing support that it needed. After several months of instability, we decided to close the project, hoping for better times to restart it. We thought it was better to finish than to drag the project out halfheartedly. Even so, we feel that this alchemy of children, art, culture, and environmental education proved to be fruitful and necessary. With all our mistakes and our successes, we believe that through the art workshops we have planted some good seeds in Kuna Yala.[10]

Creative tensions

There were tensions both within the project as well in the broader external context that impacted the project.

External Tensions

The implementation of the project created competition between the state's school system and cultural institutions. In communities like Ailigandi the school authorities and the National Institute of Culture (INAC) felt the impact of the workshops. Because of the creative and participatory methodology used in the workshops, the children's attendance dropped at school as well as at the artistic training programs offered by the Cultural Center administered by the INAC. Both institutions took their complaints to the Indigenous authorities of the Local Congress, pointing out that this was affecting the school dynamic. In another community, Carti Sugdup, the project's activities were seen to complement the public school services, and there was a good relationship between the art workshops network, the school authorities, and the Indigenous authorities.

Among educators and parents, there were two different kinds of attitudes: one of rejection of the project, and the other of support. The rejection was based on a concern for the impact of the activities on the children's scholarly achievement, because, according to some of them, the workshops did not provide for an adequate educational process. With the passing of time and dialogue, however, both sectors finally supported the art workshops.

Internal Tensions

The most central tension that arose out of the network's work originated with the creation of traditional dance groups made up of children in the community of Carti Sugdup. Community leaders refused to accept the creation of the dance groups, alleging that they encouraged a loss of control over the young women participating; they feared that dancing could lead to contact between the participants and that they could fall in love without the consent of their parents. This concern gradually disappeared thanks to the dialogue with the cultural facilitators coming from the communities where dances were permitted; this helped the community better understand the situation. Through direct dialogue with parents, the facilitators explained the importance of dance in the Kuna culture; there was little chance of lack of control over the female dancers since they were girls and their companions were of the same age. Over time the community accepted the existence of the children's dance groups.

Looking to the future

Words that challenge, words of hope, words of action—these are the words that express the future of this experience of popular education, of environmental education, of art promotion. Our creative dream is that the roots of the Kuna culture live on in the midst of changes throughout the Panamanian society. Former workshop facilitators now consider the possibilities of continuing the project in the city.

Sonia Henríquez, one of the collaborators of the art workshops network, speaks to us about continuing this experience in a new context, with the Kuna population who have migrated to Panama City:

It would be a good opportunity to build on what the Duiren Sapingan organization started. I think that these *barriadas* (Kuna settlements in the city) are not on the margins, they are not outside of our own culture. Art projects can highlight our cosmology, deepen community work, strengthen the youth who are growing within their people's culture in the city; they could help promote the revaluing of Indigenous art.

We, as women, are working with the youth, with the children. The women who live here in these urban communities have not abandoned their art, like the *molas*; they still make them. We should continue to instil in children and youth that this art comes from their own identity as a people.

We have had other experiences. Ten years ago, there were girls who lived here in the community who sang in their Kuna language. This artistic expression left a positive impact for the future of these girls who are Indigenous and will continue to be Indigenous.

In the city there is a dominant culture that is not ours. A project with youth would minimize the social problems that many families have. The youth do not have other means through which they can be taught our culture. They could dedicate time to this, instead of other things they are into. It would be a positive influence to be able to work with art, with painting . . . based on their own community, getting to know their commu-

nity's history. There are children who grow up not knowing the reasons for the internal migration, why there are these *barriadas* (slum areas); they do not know our *Comarcal* (regional) history.

An art project like this would strengthen our cultural Indigenous identity. It would give us a chance to reflect and to take stock. Now it's the city that is having the greatest influence on us. Many leaders could use art as a way to get through to the youth, to the children, so that our millennial culture can be revalued, so that they can understand that there is a history, that they are part of a rich cultural identity. This type of artistic cultural work would strengthen the organizational work that we do.

From the experience of a cultural facilitator of the children's art workshops, José Angel Colman also reflects on the future of the process and its contributions to the Kuna experience in the city:

Now many Kuna are living in the city. You see the children in the seven poor neighborhoods that surround the city. The Kuna children living in the city are very different; their relationship with the community isn't as strong as the children living on the island. As Kuna we are privileged, because of the kind of organization we have, and we don't want to lose it. But these children don't have so much experience with it. Working with children from the city you have to work in a different way. Offer them images through myths and stories, so that they can recreate their relationship with their origins.

Of course, times have changed. It's another way of being for these Kuna children living in the city. We must work with more dynamic methods. We need to study these children a bit more, so that their experience is enriched from here; we must motivate them to relate to their communities of origins. It would be a very rich experience for them, for example, if they could return to their islands during their vacation to live in the community.

We Kuna have the privilege of living in two worlds: the Indigenous world with all its richness

Kuna woman in Panama City

and the Latino world of Panama City with its concrete experiences. The world of the Kuna is spiritual, it is the world of sensations . . . of dreams. It is a world to be seen through art; for example, the design of the *molas* are an expression of the mothers and they reflect a different sensation of living in an Indigenous community. Uniting these two worlds would be enriching for the children who live in the city.

It is another moment, now as people talk about the market, about globalization. The Kuna children here are being raised within this experience of globalization, of cell phones, of the Internet. How can we combine these two worlds? Because otherwise, they will be trapped in only one world of global communications. This would be dangerous, even though it may seem like an advantage. That is, we need to know how to use technology to be able to communicate even with our Indigenous world. The future will be a new creation, a new Kuna man [person]. We must continue the experience of the children's art workshops with these young people.

The city has been transformed into a new scenario, challenging and complex, with a growing Kuna population, a community structure that survives and adapts itself, a generation of Kuna born and raised in the city who both approach and distance themselves from their culture. These are the challenges.

However, a rich experience is underway and shows us the possibility of making identity more dynamic, of strengthening organizing and community work, and of involving future generations in the world of artistic creation and expression.

See Aiban Wagua, "Civiliza Mi Corazón, Mamá," *La Tinaja Kuna* (Kuna Yala, Panama: 1987).

CHAPTER 2

THE LOST BODY

Recovering Memory—A Personal Legacy

Diane Roberts, with Heather Hermant and Lopa Sircar
Personal Legacy Project, Vancouver, Canada

Diane Roberts at Galiano Island Fathom Labs Highway residency, BC, 2006

The Personal Legacy project

Relache. Never a kinder word was spoken when, in Hervé Maxi's Haitian dance class,[1] after multiple deep bends and ballet toes, I was finally told to *relache* (. . . 2, 3, 4 . . .). I found my body challenged to its limit in that class not knowing that greater challenges lay ahead. In a repertoire class in Central African dance during my attempts to master the Zeboula, a healing dance from the Congo, my body was stressed seemingly beyond repair. These frustrations caused me to question my body's response to the differing cultural contexts. Why could I more easily recognize and adapt to the Haitian movement vocabulary over the Congolese?

I tried to reason with my muscles—explaining that the Haitian dance form, with its commingling of European and African slave dance and ritual movements, was equally as foreign to me and my experience as the movements coming from the Continent itself. My body, however, was telling a different story and after much frustration, confusion, and determination, I realized that my answers lay within the contradictions housed in this my "Antillean body." Derek Walcott describes this complex very well in his Nobel laureate speech:

> Break a vase, and the love that reassembles the fragments is stronger than that love which took its symmetry for granted when it was whole. The glue that fits the pieces is the sealing of its original shape . . . and if the pieces are disparate, ill-fitting, they contain more pain than their original sculpture, those icons and sacred vessels taken for granted in their ancestral places.[2]

The Personal Legacy work was born out of my personal longing to belong. My university training as a theater artist introduced the pressure of having to conform to what I was told to believe was a universal aesthetic. In negotiating my identity as the only black female performance student, I tried to conform and to mimic the "classical" forms. During our daily exercises there was a blanking out of self—a neutral body mask—that would, in theory, put us, as performers, in a state of readiness to transform into any character we were presented with. I soon became aware that my neutral mask with thick lips, nappy hair, and an S-curve into ample buttocks could never be neutral enough—try as I might to tuck and hold and breathe and survive. My experience of alienation in the academy of higher learning for the arts is part of the legacy I carry in my body to this day.

Since that time, things seem to have changed here in Canadian training institutions. The larger arts community continues their "long day's journey" toward embracing the *idea* of "diversity," and universities have followed through by adding special topics courses on "other" world theater forms. In the better case scenarios they have integrated their programs with contemporary arts practices from a variety of world traditions (albeit viewed through a European lens). Things have changed. So dem say. Yet still, I've witnessed young graduate "artists of color" adept at the execution of their own neutral body stance while lacking a strong sense of themselves and their personal historic bodies. As performance students they are taught to discard this self in service of the role—the exercise, the process. Yet how can one discard a thing as elusive as self when self, being often defined by place, is constantly disrupted by the unpredictability of place? The Canadian immigration process (forced or otherwise) and its multiple expressions—integration, multiculturalism, diversity, othering, separation, alienation, adaptation, reintegration, racism, and the dominant culture's shifting political and social gaze—all contribute to a fragmented consciousness.

The African storyteller has often been described as a chameleon. S/he changes with the shape of each story by bending his/her self in service. This ability to adapt one's essence—one's very being—can have both positive and negative implications. What if, for example, the story carries you across the ocean against your will in the dank and dark hold of a vessel headed for a new world? For example, adapting to this story might require you to actively and forcefully forget, minimizing the horrors of the dehumanizing journey. In this crossing the chameleon storyteller may have become the vessel, the hold, the rats, the stagnating excrement plastering the floors and walls. And yet, suppressing the screams s/he will "Speak of Rivers . . ."[3] Suppressing the stench, the whip, the oppressor's fist and dick . . . "And Still (I) Rise . . ."[4] Forgetting in the new world becomes not only a technique of survival but a right of passage.

And my story begins here. In Canada. In residues and conjecture, I imagine the unimaginable.

Far from the hold of a shit-stained vessel, I retrace a legacy that begins for me in St. Vincent. As I wrote in my Legacy research journal:

> I never knew my Grandfather. In fact, my father never knew his father. The pitchy patchy story bits in this traveling nomadic legacy touch down on the MS *Madanina* (a Caribbean cargo and transport ship), in Cane Garden, St. Vincent, at the Southern Games in Trinidad, extending to The London Underground, New York's upper west side and down south, Toronto and Montreal . . . Alexander Delmar (meaning "from the sea") Roberts, a "bush healer," a member of a covert society, had secret affairs and public embarrassments, and was believed to have been poisoned all before my father's second birthday.

Inhabiting this "reassembled" frame, just below its foundation, is an ancestral war dance between the colonizer and the colonized, between the slave master and the slave, between the European explorer and the African warrior. The battle manifests itself daily, in my mind, my hips, my knees, my feet, my ankles, my joints, my blood, my bones, my tongue . . . my being. In his Nobel laureate speech, Walcott speaks of the pain of reconstructing ill-fitting pieces and this makes sense. He speaks of sacred vessels and forgotten ancestral places and this rings a bell. He speaks of a careful re-gathering and the pain of re-membering, and my bones vibrate in recognition.

The context for the Personal Legacy work is, has been, and will continue to be the colonized body. And although I begin from a personal contextual framework, the Personal Legacy process, in its development, has revealed its universal application, for participants across backgrounds and arts disciplines, within and outside of the academy. In an academy that is becoming more and more diverse, the Personal Legacy work is a vital grounding tool for dialogue across difference.

From the inside out: Community-building opportunities

In January 2005, I met Toronto-based spoken-word artist Heather Hermant in a workshop I conducted at York University; and in May of the same year I met actor/

Diane's mother, Irva Roberts,
Grenada, West Indies, 1940

writer Lopa Sircar in an intensive voice-training course at the University of British Columbia in Vancouver. After working with Heather at York and hearing about Lopa's plans to research her own family legacy, it became clear that they should be the first Personal Legacy collaborators.

Like the Catalyst Centre's Telling Our Stories project, the Personal Legacy work has targeted emerging community artists and has been developed to address the intersection between art and social movements from specific and culturally rooted perspectives. It challenges participants to draw from the rich tapestries of their inner lives as a source of creativity and as an action toward understanding others.

The deeply personal approach has been developed over time with collaborating artist Heather Hermant. Its target group has consisted of young, emerging, and mid-career artists whose impulse to connect to ancestral ties comes from a desire to understand more deeply their present self, family, and community. Our objective has been to see the Personal Legacy tools develop into a process with many and varied applications.

The motivation behind Personal Legacy comes from our many years of witnessing the profound disconnect that so many racialized artists in Canada feel about themselves, their environment, and their cultural histories. One cannot discount as a contributing factor, the lingering effects of migration, colonization, and the forces of assimilation.

The Personal Legacy process attempts to address this oft-times alienating factor by providing routes to anchor participants in their own stories. The process helps catalyze dialogue within families and communities, and strengthens artists' sense of themselves in community. Like a porthole to the past, Personal Legacy helps participants discover and make sense of the histories stored within. For participants it can be an ancestral anchor that grounds them, and gives them confidence while they develop as artists, facilitators, and community leaders.[5]

Developing the process

Personal Legacy is a physical/dramaturgical process based on a combination of West/Central African dance, ritual, and story traditions—where the teller/dancer and the story/event are in a dynamic and changing relationship. Evolving out of these traditions, the Personal Legacy work is an embodied process exploring Ancestry. Originally designed for an acting course, its aim was to bring the actor into alignment with his or her authentic cultural-

historic body as a grounding tool for subsequent character development work. At the center of this process is the acknowledgment that everything we need to draw on for inspiration is stored in our bodies as memory. The Personal Legacy work provides an entryway to access ancestral memory. In its evolution, this work has revealed itself to be a vitally important self-discovery/recovery tool that exposes questions of shifting identity during transmigration.

This work is not in and of itself unique. Ancestral recovery is the foundation on which many Indigenous cultural traditions have been built. African and Afrisporic traditions such as Cuban Santeria, Yorubuan Lokumi, Haitian Voudoun all draw on the power of ancestral spirits, creating songs, dances, and visual art to express and demonstrate the continual flow of energy between worlds. Jamaican Kumina religious followers and Trinidadian Shouter Baptists practice specific rites that recognize death as a passage from one physical form to another. For the Shona people of Zimbabwe, ancestral spirits are a source of comfort as well as the cornerstone of religious activity.

What makes the Personal Legacy work unique is its application in a cross-cultural or "multisporic" (rather than "diasporic") setting. Although I draw heavily on my knowledge (empirical, experiential, and instinctive) of Afrisporic traditions, the exercises themselves—in that they demand attention to one's own definition of root culture—makes the work universal and accessible.

The process defined

In the initial stage of the Personal Legacy process, participants are mentored through conducting research into an ancestor at least two generations away, through archival research, family, and/or community interviews. Using exercises developed to awaken sense and memory, participants learn technical and physical skills necessary to work in the cultural memories that are stored in their bodies.

With the aid of an outside witness (another participant), the facilitator guides

Diane Roberts and Lopa Sircar, Galiano Island, 2006

the participant toward a first ancestral meeting. S/he will live inside (without using words) a compelling moment in the life of his or her ancestor. The challenge for the performer is to stay in the body and world of the ancestor for five to twelve minutes without trying to make anything happen. A strong and dynamic relationship between the external witness (outside observer) and internal witness (performer) is vitally important when reconstructing the experience post-embodiment. The dialogue following the embodiment mirrors back the experience of the performer and the witness uncovers deeper levels of the Legacy subject's narrative.

There are three phases to the work: the research phase, the embodiment phase, and the group discussion / feedback phase.

Choose a person in your family at least two generations away whom you have never met or have met only once.

Each of these phases requires a commitment on the part of the researcher/performer to enter the contradictory world of investigative research and embodied knowing.

It may take you time to identify the person you'd like to work with or you may find that someone jumps into your mind right away. Follow your instincts . . .

After an initial research phase to generate a character profile, the researcher/performer enters the studio for the first embodiment guided by the facilitator and an outside witness. At this stage the archival research is put to one side and serves as a map for the ensuing bodily process.

. . . The magic arises when your Legacy subject leads you instead of the other way around.

A significant principle governing the process is the dynamic relationship between the subject, the performer, the facilitator/animator, and the outside witness.

Imagine your Legacy person across the way from you in an environment where you might find them: a field, a room, a parlor, a seashore . . .

There are three key positions on a spiral that, when viewed from above, travel inward toward the center point or "source." The source represents the Legacy subject. They include the inner loop, the mid-to-outer loop, and the outermost loop. Through the process, the performer attempts to travel along the innermost loop—closing in on the subject/source.

Imagine your Legacy person moving around in this environment oblivious to the gaze of an outside spectator . . .

As facilitator, I find myself tentatively (if not instinctively) traveling one loop behind the performer—testing distance, approach, and duration while questioning, lingering, mirroring breath patterns, and shifting body weight, listening for moments to test and provoke as well as moments to allow and support.

Imagine being greeted with the warm smile of your Legacy person. Imagine meeting face to face for the first time . . .

The witness remains stationary on the outermost loop of the spiral. Her vitally important role in the exercise is to observe and record key moments of intersection between the facilitator, performer, and source, and to interpret through feedback her own experiences as outside observer. Collaborating artist Lopa Sircar describes the value of the witness in her research journal during a Vancouver workshop in November 2006:

Perhaps the most valuable aspect of exploring with a witness is that the witness allows me (as performer) to dive deep into my work with the knowledge that details of movement, breath, eye focus, text—the keys to profound embodied storytelling—will be documented and offered back to me, as the delicious and inspiring fruits of my labor.

Relying on intuition, inside and outside, I, as facilitator, must stay deeply immersed in the discomfort, yet outside enough to guide the performer through the darkness toward a window, a lighted doorway . . . And still, I witness my own voice shifting according to the needs of the Legacy subject.

Let me describe three different moments—one with Lopa and her grandfather, one with Heather embodying Esther Brandeau, a historical figure discovered in work with her great-great-grandmother, and the third my own embodiment of my grandfather Delmar.

During Lopa's embodiment, I felt my voice shift naturally in response to her grandfather's presence—a charismatic and formidable character with a powerful and dignified poise—one who, though gentle and kind, commanded respect and deference to his well-earned power. From the moment he arrived I felt myself respond like a gentle wind, quiet and inquisitive—almost childlike.

Working with Esther embodied in Heather, my voice was stronger, fuller—responsive to Esther's vigilance. I

Danielle Smith, Toronto Personal Legacy Workshop, 2007

quietly observed myself add weight to my voice. I felt the physical and semiconscious shift from my own gentle tone into a more grounded and directed one. Esther's response was often suspicious and guarded, perhaps because, as Heather described, "[my] questions were too close to what she had known as interrogation." I found myself struggling to negotiate the silencing land mines I so often stumbled into.

When Heather facilitated my own embodiment, she experienced, as she describes, "the intimidating confidence, almost arrogance" of Delmar, "a very big man physically, and clearly someone who expected to be in charge." Documentation became difficult for this embodiment because Delmar seemed threatened by the camera. "It was like walking on eggshells, but I knew how important it would be for Diane to see his energy and taking up of space in her own body."

Imagine . . .

In the academy, the Personal Legacy work has been well received. Participants have reported the "eerie" feeling of having not only touched the core of their Legacy subject but also, surprisingly, of having opened up hidden truths within themselves. The Personal Legacy work is professed to be not only a foundational tool for performance but also a leveling ground for discussions of culture and difference—discussions that have, in the past, been labeled taboo because of their perceived incendiary, isolating, or alienating effect in the classroom. This leveling effect has not only been vitally important for the initial target group of this exercise (racialized artists), but for all concerned.

I've experienced a history of emotional estrangement from some of the men in my family. For this very reason, it was a profound opportunity and experience to initiate a relationship with my grandfather. His defining success was in education, an area of my life which I can experience as thrilling at times, but more often, as a difficult struggle because of the combined legacy and pressure of expected academic excellence and disregard for the emotional struggle caused by the intersecting systems of oppression within educational institutions, a microcosm of our larger world.

—Danielle Smith, Caribbean Women's Studies, University of Toronto, Personal Legacy Workshop Toronto, March 2007

The Arrivals project: A Personal Legacy exchange

Despite its obvious applications in a training context, the power of the work is best demonstrated in its artistic and community development applications, especially within the "multicultural mosaic" that popularly defines the Canadian experience. It addresses what is often touched on but rarely explored in our work as community development workers: the importance of family heritage as an influencing force. The Personal Legacy work, using all aspects of self—the emotional, the spiritual, the physical, and the intellectual—not only encourages intergenerational exchange but uses this exchange as a catalyzing force for personal and community development, by plunging the performer into the realm of unconscious knowing.

During one incarnation of the classroom exercise, I challenged my students (who had already embodied

The Charlie Family, urban ink's "From Where We Speak Project," Galiano Island, 2008

their own ancestors) to go one step further by exchanging Legacy subjects. In other words: student A would embody student B's ancestor and vice versa. The students embraced the challenge, learning from each other the outside bodily habits: paying attention to weight, balance, walk, and physical habits, and then attempting to imagine the inner life of their newly inherited Legacy subject. The catch was that to truly inhabit their new character they had to find their own central being within the shell of another. The implications of this kind of exchange, almost too huge to contemplate, are currently being explored through the first stages of the Arrivals project Personal Legacy Exchange.

We believe that the Arrivals project Personal Legacy Exchange addresses a key challenge for community arts: apprenticing locally based emerging artists to first work with their own communities, and then to foster networks among such artists so that they may serve as key facilitators of meaningful intercommunity exchange and joint initiatives. The overall aim of the project is mentorship of a new generation of community artists, with a particular emphasis on empowering artists from diverse socioeconomic and cultural backgrounds who work in and come from "underserved"' communities.[6]

It is important to note that we see the Arrivals project Personal Legacy Exchange as a proactive resistance to the agenda of mosaic multiculturalism—now named "diversity." In our Canadian context, definitions of "diversity" and "community development" continually assume the centering of the dominant culture despite well meaning and often superficial liberal references to "our Aboriginal friends" or "newcomers." Focusing on the responsibility to know our ancestral paths and/or personal histories levels the ground in these contexts, removing the temptation to cast ourselves as rescue workers or to privilege ourselves over marginalized communities.

For aspiring community artists who might feel distanced from their own histories and communities, the Arrivals project fosters access to their histories, to transformative ways of working with their communities, and to opportunities for building those communities. And it gives communities access to arts opportunities facilitated by locally based emerging community artists.[7]

For me, community art is grounded in identity and place. Both are transient, and the focus is usually on the future. Personal Legacy has made me realize that without knowing your past, you cannot embrace your future.

—Stephanie Archambault, York University CAP Program, student participant, Personal Legacy Workshop, Toronto, March 2007

Emerging Legacy projects

The Personal Legacy work is a spiritual journey, but it is also a house of techniques that can be honed to a high level of skill. Just like one can learn to dream with skill, a skill highly esteemed in many cultures, one can learn to enter an embodiment, and various positions at once: I am Esther, I am Heather witnessing Heather as Esther, I am Heather facilitating as Heather waits for/with Esther, asking the right questions in a fusion of languages to lead to the information embodiment offers.

—Heather Hermant, research journal, Toronto

In June 2006, during a residency at urban ink production's Fathom Labs retreat center on Galiano Island, British Columbia, collaborating artists Heather Hermant, Lopa Sircar, and I gathered to workshop and document the beginning stages of Heather's work, *ribcage: this wide passage*, and Lopa's piece, *The Vermillion Project*, as well as to further explore the techniques of the Personal Legacy work.

Heather's subject was drawn from the historic crossing of Esther Brandeau, said to be the first Jewish person to land on Canadian soil, who arrived passing as Christian and male.

The first person to call me in the Legacy work was my great-great-grandmother, a daughter of orthodox religious Jews in a *shtetl* in what is now Belarus. She had been married off to a much older widower when she was barely twenty. She later rejected this fate, and with their infant son, walked back to her parents' village. Later that son stowed

Heather Hermant, Galiano Island, 2006

Lopa Sircar, urban ink Arrivals Project, Toronto, 2009

away on a ship that landed in New Brunswick. This is our family foundation lore. Researching her meant reading Jewish Canadian history, where inevitably I found another defiant character, Esther Brandeau.

—Heather Hermant

Lopa's subject came from her interaction with four key family members who made themselves known to her during her trip to India.

Being Canadian by birth but Bengali by nature, the root of my impulse to create this work stems from my curiosity to delve into that part of me where my ancestors continue to dwell—in gesture, body language, pronunciations, breath—a multitude of unconscious and conscious Bengalisms that are present in me in spite of my largely "white" upbringing. I have chosen three Personal Legacy subjects on whose lived experience I base The Vermillion Project.

—Lopa Sircar

The workshop revealed uncanny similarities—between the two stories and between their individual journeys toward realizing the projects—that could not be denied. Although our task in the Fathom Labs workshop wasn't to explore the exchange of Legacy stories, there was an irrefutable intersection between the two life stories that tapped into a larger archetypical landscape—larger than their individual circumstances.

Finding Esther and recognizing in it a queer story was like finally finding an anchor for myself, queerness and part-Jewishness brought together from their unanchored, unclearly separate positions within. It's not surprising that Esther has become a vehicle for my family to talk about our history. She is an excuse for stories. Through late night conversations with older relatives, I understand for the first time the reality of diaspora in my several generations' assimilated life.

—Heather Hermant

I've spent this evening hearing about my grandfather's family—like four hundred years ago. . . . I can feel my blood clawing its way back through a larger, global history—red and bulging with life and potential—a sense that I can stretch backwards and forwards in equal distances—that I am a part of a continuum. . . . My grandfather lived what he believed: do your work . . . do good deeds and expect nothing. He writes in his book, from Tagore, that "it is our past that pushes us into our future." I am starting to see how that can be true.

—*Lopa Sircar*

The governing principle here is that if you have the compassion and courage to inhabit fully the skin and to touch the soul of an "other" with all of his/her strengths and faults, you may be one step closer to truly embodying the concept of cross-cultural understanding. In a community development context, this kind of exchange can have enormous repercussions.

Ways of knowing: A transformative collaborative process

To be drawn to the Legacy work means you bring with you not only a legacy project but also a desire to work from a culturally specific performance tradition. This is a vitally important aspect of the Personal Legacy work. Since the context, described earlier as the colonized body, extends beyond the personal and into the universal, participating artists have an opportunity to explore what Gloria Anzaldua describes as *Nepantla*: "It is a liminal space, a space where you are not this or that but where you are changing . . . you are in a kind of transition . . . in the midst of transformation."[8]

The Personal Legacy work drops the performer inside this transformative space and asks her to hover there, in a state of waiting.

During the embodiment process, the subject needs the facilitator to guide her through the unknown, give her the confidence to wait for the unexpected. The witness remembers what the embodier forgets of her experience when she enters the embodiment fully. It is a three-way col-

Lopa Sircar, Galiano Island, 2006

laboration. There were times (when Lopa, Diane, and I were first working as a team) that Lopa or I would be unable to remember where we had been in our embodiments, what we had done with our bodies. Our outside witnesses would give back to us gestures, movements, words that we had brought without remembering.

The more I have worked alone with the process, being in all three positions (external witness, facilitator, internal witness) simultaneously, the more I have realized that I am never the Legacy subject entirely. I am in a negotiated state of approaching. I carry my outside I/eye, and I need this outside (perspective) to help me wait and risk, and to hold the place for me to retreat to (safely) when the work inside becomes too much, as it often has been. Too much

Heather Hermant performing "ribcage: this wide passage", 2008

violence, too much holding the body in a physically draining, constant state of vigilance, too much exertion as someone who was physically much stronger than me.

—*Heather Hermant*

And, as uncomfortable as it often tends to be, I listen for hints and clues and the ripening first fruits of a legacy once lost to time and forgotten gravestones.

Risks and rewards

There is an element of risk in this work. The unknown outcome always seems to initially resemble a large and dark cavernous valley—ominous and intimidating. Right before entering the exercise many rational and irrational fears arise for those in the roles of the embodier, the witness, and the facilitator. Managing the fear is an important part of the journey. When to push through, when to listen, when to hold on, and when to let go—all are in delicate balance. As I wrote in my legacy journal during our 2006 session on Galiano Island:

> First Day of Embodiment:
>
> I'm nervous. No need to be. I've done this so many times before.
>
> I'm scared.
>
> Of what?
>
> Not living up to the memory.
>
> Not trusting the exercise.
>
> Not being a good enough witness.
>
> Not being enough.
>
> Lopa begins. Just relax and feel your breath and allow your body to sink into a cloud. And the music begins. Lopa breathing in the picture of her grandfather and her grandfather living in the space she created for him and all of a sudden he's no longer in the distance but he opens his arms in a welcoming embrace. The form has been broken. The embrace was too fast. It was meant to happen after a full ten minutes of observation. How do I back track? And then I see it was meant to happen because the release of tears melts away the anxiety and she sinks deeper into the lived memory of his embrace. And memory, like water washes through, carving a passage to worlds gone by.

In addition, the therapeutic and/or spiritual aspects of the Personal Legacy journey are unmistakable and need to be respected and honored.

> It would be nice to know how different cultural practices of "channeling," for lack of a better word, deal with this challenge. It is making me more and more aware that legacy work in any depth has to be done with great care, and cannot be done with just anyone . . .

—*Heather Hermant (email)*

My desire to run from these glaring aspects speaks not only to the power this work has to reach beyond its initial impulse but also to my instinct to try to control this reach.

Hi Heather, The first thing I'd like to say is that this work is artistic work. Without diminishing the significance and profundity of your experience we need to be clear about that. We are not channeling and we are not engaging in ceremonial or shamanic practice . . .

—*Diane Roberts (email)*

And still, its conscious ties to African artistic practice make this connection undeniable.

. . . I do agree that there are some spiritual aspects to the work that we've sort of stumbled onto (or into). . . . Now having said that, it would be inaccurate to say that we *stumbled* upon these aspects since my attempt to work within an African aesthetic where spiritual practice and arts practice are often intertwined is so central to the process . . .

—*Diane Roberts (email)*

I ask myself, how is this work tied to possession as seen in the traditions of Voudoun, Lokumi, or Santeria?[9] The host (performer) seems to be mounted or inhabited by the living spirit of the ancestor. The ancestor, choosing the time and place and how his/her story will be told is welcomed by his/her host (the performer) with a warm embrace and in that moment when time and place converge, we all realize we've moved into another reality—another world.

Even with these glaring similarities, there are different levels of entry.

I ask her, "What is this secret?" I want to know what happened, what she hasn't told me. I am suddenly made very physically aware that I cannot ask this question; I am forced out of the setting, I find myself running across the studio unable to look back at where I had been standing. The studio is warm but I am cold and terrified. I have tested a limit. For some of what I am shown, I can witness but I cannot ask questions about what I

have seen, and I don't have permission to tell. I am learning to recognize my sense of entitlement to know everything. We cannot know everything.

—*Heather Hermant, research journal, Toronto 2006*

Some subjects will allow entry into the unconscious, will allow entry into their souls, dreams, hidden memories, while others will only allow a guarded entry into surface events. It is up to the performer/host, with the help of the outside witness, to discern the difference. This balance, this element of control that must be respected in the Personal Legacy work, speaks to the tension between holding on and letting go that tends to prevail in our work as popular educators. The bond that is developed between the facilitator, the witness, and the performer is based on mutual trust and a full recognition that at each position on the Legacy spiral there is great risk. The reward at the end of a session has been, more often than not, sheer exhaustion, then blissful confusion and finally deep understanding.

Doubts and coincidences

You may be disappointed to hear that while I am having an amazing and insightful time here, my ideas have become less clear, not more.

—*Lopa Sircar, research journal, Bengal, India, January 2006*

There is a certain uncertainty about the Legacy process—like stepping into the abyss and this process is as important as the final product. Unable to predict where the work will lead, we enter the dark spaces with a faith that our journey to the other side will reap much fruit: possibilities, insights, artistic source material, text bits, image strands . . .

I discovered that the archive has incorrectly filed several documents pertaining to Esther. I found them by total sheer mysterious accident, I just happened to stop the microfilm reel at just the right moment . . .

—*Heather Hermant, research journal, National Archives, Ottawa*

Zainab Amadahy, urban ink Arrivals Project, Toronto, 2009

Some of the doubts that arise in the work can be gateways to further understanding. Our work is to stay open and enter this *Nepantla*—this liminal space of knowing and unknowing.

I'm here and not here. I'm experiencing an altered consciousness—I know I've tapped the unconscious . . . but have I tapped the ancestral? From where do we learn to listen? Have we really discovered the profound breath open welcoming of the ancestral voice or is it just coincidence?

—Diane Roberts, research journal,
Galiano Island, British Columbia

What do we do with the "inch work"? Where do these minute internal movements lead us? Do they point toward a greater w/hole? How do we know we're headed in the right direction? Are these found impulses connected to the subject/source or to our own habitual patterns or preexisting assumptions?

I am making tiny but important headway . . . what I continue to struggle with is what Canadian novelist Larissa Lai was saying when I went to hear her read, about how the novel as a form is oppressive because it demands a through-line, and that what I need to do with this project is resist the through-line and instead offer the dead ends and possibilities and searches that I have been on.

—Heather Hermant (email)

Despite the doubts, one thing I know for certain is that the Personal Legacy work makes history live again. It absolves the sinners, exposes the demons, personalizes deified heroes and brings them down to human level. The Personal Legacy work is a gateway from the outside to the inside, from the *there* and *then* to the *here* and *now*, from the *political* to the *personal*, from the *you* to *me*, from the *them* to *us*.

PART II

Transforming Urban Spaces

From Postcolonial Neighborhoods to Public Squares

INTRODUCTION

An evolving analytical framework

From the start, we meant to use the creative tensions first elaborated by VIVA! partners, and introduced in Part I, not as dichotomies but as dialectics to be understood in dynamic relationship to each other. At our second annual gathering in Panama, however, we began to question whether our framework of creative tensions ultimately reproduces the dichotomous thinking that we claim to challenge. We seemed caught between the linear and dualistic thinking of Western Enlightenment worldviews and Indigenous cosmovisions that were more cyclical, holistic, and integrated. After three days of hearing about and analyzing the local projects, we engaged in a process of *sistematización*; out of this grounded theorizing emerged a new model in the form of a spiral, which resonated more with non-Western visions that most inspire us.[1]

We proposed two interrelated spirals, one to synthesize the core substantive focus of our research and the other to synthesize the methodology; in other words, we reframed both the "what" and the "how" of our project in the form of spirals. After a year of engagement in our projects, it had become clear that our central substantive interest was transformation: historical and cultural recovery that uses art as a transformative process to represent peoples' stories, ultimately feeding popular education for social change; this is illustrated in the first spiral.

In a second spiral, we identified the key features of our methodology: one that was integrated and holistic (ecological and interdisciplinary), that

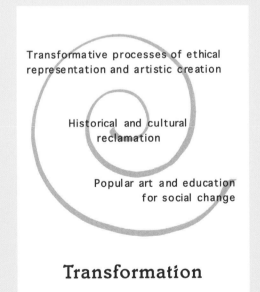

Transformative processes of ethical representation and artistic creation

Historical and cultural reclamation

Popular art and education for social change

Transformation

was built on intergenerational dialogue (engaging young artists with elders), and that was explicitly intercultural, addressing issues of equity both within our projects and within own transnational collaboration.

While the spiral allowed us to revisit our original framework, we didn't abandon the creative tensions altogether, in fact, many projects kept identifying their own particular tensions as a way of engaging the more difficult questions and sticky moments that are all grist for learning in popular education. The fact that these two approaches straddle the line between critical social thought and postmodern challenges and cautions perhaps represents a murky reality—that we find ourselves in the fertile interstices of the two.

Transformative possibilities in urban spaces

We live in an era of the "global city." The increasing migration to urban contexts all over the world—whether a result of war and displacement, corporate globalization and neoliberal trade, political or environmental exile, the industrialization of agriculture and economic desperation—has dramatically changed the populations of cities. Recent projections in Toronto paint a picture of a population in 2031, for example, made up of 67 percent visible minorities.[2] Several of the VIVA! projects in our exchange unfolded in cities with populations ranging from five million (Toronto) to thirty-five million (Mexico City).

As Maggie Hutcheson, VIVA! partner, videographer, researcher, and participant in the Toronto-based Jumblies

Intergenerational
- dialogue
- oral histories in many artistic forms
- internships

Integrated and holistic
- integration of body, mind, spirit
- transdisciplinary
- ecological vision

Intercultural
- diverse geographic and political contexts
- ethnicity, race, gender, age
- organizations
- urban/rural

Creative tensions

Panama City viewed from the old city

Theatre project, suggests in her doctoral work on place-based public art in the "displaced city":

> Underwritten in the ecological and architectural landscapes of cities, as well as in the untold stories of past and present inhabitants are histories of displacement, migration, settlement, social struggles, and ideological and material cultural shifts.[3]

Hutcheson's notion of "displacement" refers to myriad historical processes: the colonial ravaging of Indigenous lands and cultures; the arrival of migrants for political,

economic, and cultural reasons; the gentrification of neighborhoods that destroys and displaces low-income and racialized communities; the emergence of a "creative cities" discourse that favors those with social and economic capital,[4] and so forth.

She cites Jane M. Jacobs in suggesting that cities and neighborhoods are ideal lenses through which to examine "the (post)colonial politics of identity and place."[5] As we suggested in the introduction to this volume, communities are neither monolithic nor fixed in time or place, so an examination of community arts projects in transnational cities must engage the constant reconstruction of community and identities, including the hybrid forms of representation they create out of the cauldron of diverse intersecting cultures.

In the next three chapters, the integrated, interdisciplinary, and intercultural processes of community-engaged art projects in urban contexts (Toronto and Guadalajara) are examined by VIVA! partners. As reflected in the second spiral, there are new dialogues across differences of race/ethnicity, age, gender, and class; these encounters are facilitated by art-making practices that embrace diverse ways of knowing and a wide range of cultural expression. The deeper aims of the three projects vary, if examined around the interrelated themes of the first spiral. While they all involve historical and cultural reclamation in some form, they also challenge any monolithic notion of that process, and engage in constant reinvention of cultures and creation of hybrid practices (embodying the third creative tension between cultural reclamation and cultural reinvention). They all affirm the transformative value of art-making, but some are more consciously integrating those processes into popular education or movements for social change.

The Jumblies Theatre's Bridge of One Hair project, for example, involved research into the west Toronto neighborhood that revealed it has a buried Indigenous history, and was settled in the early 1900s by the British and Irish whose wealthy homes face a complex of low-income high-rise apartments filled by an influx in recent decades of immigrants and refugees from Somalia, the Caribbean, Korea, and Eastern Europe. The economic disparity, racial tensions, and diverse cultural practices in the neighborhood mirror the process of globalization in postcolonial cities around the world. The Bridge of One Hair project embraces these contradictions and works to

represent them from the bottom up, transforming the towers into sites of multiple aesthetics, unusual connections, and limitless creativity. Over the three years of the project, as many as thirty artists were brought to work with residents in many mediums, from photo voice with youth to sewing with Somalian seniors; the artists, for the most part, are outsiders to the community, but work to tap the creativity and uncover the hidden stories of residents, who draw on their memories of other places while struggling to root themselves in a new place. Artistic director Ruth Howard discusses the creative tensions within the project, and insists that it is driven by the art-making that creates a space for people to confirm their own shifting identities and connect across differences.

left: *Shawan Johnson and Renwick Henry,*
Arts4All, Toronto

below: *Eli Howard in "Bridge of One Hair" production*

Another Toronto-based project, Telling Our Stories, trained young artists of color to animate youth through many diverse artistic practices. In contrast to the Jumblies approach, this project primarily works with artists who are insiders to their communities. It is not only about claiming public space in the physical sense but also about claiming cultural space for the voices of youth who have been typically marginalized. The lion's share of funding for community arts in urban centers like Toronto is aimed at youth arts projects, and there are new fusions of cultural expression emerging through multiple grassroots initiatives. Some would question, however, whether this is primarily a form of social control (often funded by crime prevention or social service units), keeping youth off the streets and occupying them temporarily, before they return to their unemployed and despairing state. In promoting the methodology of popular education (which is also built upon a spiral model), the Catalyst Center brings a strong political analysis that encourages artists to consider these broader social forces that shape what is possible within marginalized communities. The conversations between artists and young participants in the spin-off projects were as much about breaking silences and challenging power as they were about introducing and creating new forms of artistic expression. The aim is ultimately to create art that contributes to social justice.

The third project is even more explicitly political in its efforts to bring together countercultural youth, social activists, and artists who challenge both economic and political power. Its location, Guadalajara, Mexico, the second largest city in Mexico, epitomizes the global cities of the South, burgeoning in size and increasingly integrated into the neoliberal economy. Tianguis Cultural, however, represents resistance to this agenda by globalizing social movements that are challenging the very basis of that economy and promoting progressive values in a very conservative Catholic city. As a cultural marketplace that brings together two hundred exhibitors weekly, it eschews imported commercial products and promotes handmade crafts, creative artistic and musical activity, as well as critical discussion across social issues and movements. Heavily influenced by global culture and antiglobalization social movements, it is youth driven, but welcomes diverse cultures and generations, promulgates countercultural practices, and nurtures cross-sectoral alliances. The current struggle between

Che Guevara, icon of social activism in the community space of Tianguis Cultural

the Tianguis and the municipal government epitomizes the struggle for public space everywhere, where private-sector interests dominate and governments collude.

In fact, the blurring of the boundaries of the public and the private spheres can be witnessed through all three projects discussed in this section.

CHAPTER 3

OUT OF THE TUNNEL THERE CAME TEA

Jumblies Theatre's Bridge of One Hair Project

Ruth Howard
Jumblies Theatre, Toronto, Canada

When you set out to make art "for, about, and with the people" who live in a certain place; when you claim, furthermore, that "everyone is welcome!"; and when you happen to live in Toronto, then certain things follow. I founded Jumblies Theatre in 2001. The name Jumblies comes from a poem by nineteenth-century British nonsense poet Edward Lear, about creatures called "the Jumblies," who cheerfully go "to sea in a sieve." Jumblies Theatre consists of myself as artistic director; a core group of staff members and associated artists; a fluctuating assembly of other artists; and also a large assortment of participants, mostly volunteer. My work, and, thus, the work of Jumblies, is inspired largely by the British community play movement (as developed by the Colway Theatre Trust, now Claque Theatre, and brought to Canada by Dale Hamilton in 1990), which engages full towns or neighborhoods in large-scale productions about their histories and issues. I

Something that I thought about constantly while I was at the VIVA! gathering in Chiapas was the influence that context has on people. It was my first time really being outside of my own society, and feeling how deeply language, culture, food, landscape, climate, religion, architecture all constantly shape how we understand what's going on around us, how we think about and see the world. There were many people at the gathering, all from different geographical and philosophical places—working diligently, openly and critically to communicate to each other about the work we were doing, which was making art with people in many different ways. I was surprised to learn that there isn't a word for "community arts" in Spanish. Do we need one? I was confronted by many underlying assumptions that we all carry around inside us, and when these assumptions collided with the assumptions that underlay other contexts they became almost like canyons—cavernous and perilous to cross. I teetered on the edge of many of mine, trying not to fall in.   —*Noah Kenneally*

have adapted, adhered to, and departed from this model, while moving through several multiyear residencies in Toronto: employing artists from varied disciplines and backgrounds, creating new works to reflect the specific locality, combining the power of theater on an epic scale with intimate art-making, welcoming everyone who wants to take part and bridging differences of language, culture, ability, age, and class.[1]

In Toronto, Canada's largest city with over four million residents, almost half of whom are visible minorities, the challenges of this work are intense. Jumblies' 2004–2007 residency in a west-end Toronto neighborhood reflects this diversity: settled by immigrants from Great Britain in the 1900s, Etobicoke has been transformed in recent decades by newcomers, particularly from Eastern Europe, the Caribbean, Korea, and Somalia. Housed temporarily in Mabelle subsidized high-rises, face-to-face with more affluent and older homes, Jumblies has, at the time of writing (2006), completed two years of a project in partnership with Montgomery's Inn (a museum commemorating the first Anglo-Irish settlers) and Toronto Community Housing (where the most recent settlers live).

Our overall Jumblies' process follows overlapping phases of research and development, creation, production, and legacy. Allocating at least a year for each of these

left: *Mabelle high-rise, Toronto Community Housing*
below: *Fabric collage of high-rises in Mabelle complexes, 2006*

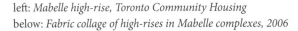

phases allows our company and the local people to become acquainted gradually, and for a meaningful creative and social process to ensue. Activities are introduced and sustained with various groups, and opportunities are sought and invented to cut across categories defined by age, culture, or economics. Artists and residents exchange, collect, and create stories, imagery, traditions, and themes, whether through recorded interviews, theater exercises, social rituals, or visual arts games.

As material accumulates, a core of artists draw from it to shape a new work of art, generally performance-based with strong visual elements. Although our process is highly collaborative, it is not a collective creation, but contains a structure and hierarchy of authorship and decision-making both like and unlike that of Western theater. The production and performance process is, likewise, both like and unlike that of a regular professional theater production.

The Etobicoke project has a particular directive to connect people across small distances but wide economic and cultural rifts. That this was a daunting task was clear from the start, and has only been substantiated by our two-year residency in the area. The tensions between different cultural groups within the public housing buildings, as well as between the public housing tenants and the nearby business and home-owning communities are overt and often disturbing. What makes this truly challenging is the project's commitment to engage with everyone, and, while bringing to the forefront the nonprivileged stories and traditions, to build bridges rather than take sides. The uniting of mismatched elements, the way it stretches our limits and forces all of us involved both to question and affirm our own roles, backgrounds, and values is the stuff of art. This is what drew me to the project in the first place: standing beside Montgomery's Inn and taking in at a glance the posh houses along Mimico Creek and the subsidized high-rises looming across Islington. Such incongruous elements are irresistible: impossible to connect except across the magical bridges that we make.

We are currently heading on a dizzying trajectory toward a large-scale production in April 2007, which, to further complicate things, will take place, not within the host community, but in a downtown Toronto art space, the Harbourfront Centre, as part of their Fresh Ground commissioning program and a major international theater festival: New World Stage. My fellow artists and I are, thus, in no way contemplating this process and its "creative tensions" from a detached vantage point, but from a vortex of flux, uncertainty, inventiveness, and trust. Through the first stages of the project our Jumblies team has moved from the outskirts of this community to being ensconced, implicated, blamed, and appreciated in its vibrant and complex midst, and from here we send these reflections.

Altogether, the project has employed over thirty artists to engage with over three hundred people. The production involved over 120 performers, more than half of them from the Mabelle housing complex and area.

> Participating in the VIVA! meeting in Chiapas has carried over into my work in Toronto. It involved enormous effort, patience, and trust. The intensity of our brief time forged new connections with people I am still learning from. I came back to Canada with a renewed sense of engagement and humility; with questions about how to become more sensitive to dynamics of power, such as race and class; and with an affirmation that clear communication and transparency in planning and decision-making are key to health and inclusiveness in art projects that engage communities. I think I came home more patient with the process, and with more trust in my own abilities.
> —Noah Kenneally

How tightly something is stretched

The project's title image, "Bridge of One Hair," comes from a favorite fairy tale of mine, "Mollie Whuppie." Mollie is a plucky young girl. When she and her two timid sisters are abandoned in the wilderness by poverty-stricken parents, she leads them through the house of a cannibalistic giant, carries them safely across a "bridge of

Miriam of the VIVA! Youth Singers, 2007

one hair," and then returns several times to steal treasures from the giant. Happily, the title image turns out to be an apt metaphor not only for the project itself and its many impossible crossings but for the VIVA! project's theme of "creative tensions." Looking up "tension," I find "mental worry or emotional strain that makes natural relaxed behavior impossible"; "a state of wariness, mistrust, controlled hostility, or fear of hostility felt by countries, groups or individuals in their dealings with one another"; "the way that opposing elements or characters clash or interact interestingly with each other in a literary work"; and "how tightly something such as a wire, string, thread or a muscle is stretched."[2]

This seems, in fact, like a fairly thorough inventory of the emotional and creative experiences in our community-engaged artwork. The tightly drawn thread is the definition that relates best to the "creative tension" notion: the necessary tightness for the seemingly impossible crossing.

Throughout the process, we constantly pose questions. The answers—the impossible bridges—lie, if anywhere, in the art-making; if they could easily be paraphrased, then perhaps we would not be artists at all.

Drops in the bucket

To start with the obvious macro tension, our work exists within an awareness of multiple social inequalities. A community such as Mabelle places the artists in the unusual (for most of us) position of being the more wealthy and privileged parties, as well as of representing, relatively speaking, the dominant cultural world. This awareness of privilege is hard for our artists to exist comfortably within. Moreover, because of Jumblies' emphasis on a strong guiding artistic vision, this dilemma cannot easily be evaded by an approach of self-effacing facilitation, even assuming that this were ever possible.

Mabelle youth in Bridge of One Hair workshop, 2006

The desire to work outside of specialized art places is itself tension-inducing, since adequate space is fundamental not only to doing a good art-making job but also to including people. In our abandonment, albeit with good reason, of already established arts places, we wander into somewhat unviable territory. In pursuit of space and other types of support, we find ourselves yoked with institutions whose values and modes of operation may diverge from our own: schools, business associations, heritage organizations, churches, and social service agencies. As project leaders, we also find ourselves straddling the not-entirely synchronized desires and agendas of these diverse partners.

Then there is the tension between the particularly ephemeral nature of theater versus the pressure (internal and external) to create something that lasts. One of the innovations in Jumblies' residency projects has been to include a funded postproduction year. The Etobicoke project will be the second project that has included such a "final" phase. The result in our previous project, was that, because the community impact and desire to continue was huge and because Jumblies was deeply implicated (had moved from the outside to the inside), there was nothing "final" about it at all, and we are still negotiating the fact that "sustainability" seems to mean never getting to leave. This raises many questions. What happens when a community arts project is over? How does one preserve its memory? Or prolong its life? Or should we? How long counts as permanent? And when is transience okay?

Yet another overall tension concerns the limits to 'inclusion': both how to accommodate the reality that some people are too truly disruptive and antisocial to include and the aesthetic implications of saying "absolutely everyone is welcome," and meaning it, or trying

> A question that arises . . . is in what ways can older artists from the dominant culture continue to thrive artistically and financially in our field while using our privilege and experience to make way for artists who are from the marginalized communities where we are working in order to develop the field to a fuller extent?
> —*Loree Lawrence*

to. Finally, the tension between control and abandon is one that operates at all levels of the work: from its broadest conception to its tiniest detail. It is both a matter of choice—as artists we want to encourage participants to bring their own creative energies to a process while also maintaining our own visions that enrich the process and outcomes—and of inevitability—unpaid and untrained participants are unpredictable and hard to marshal toward a goal that is too precisely pre-imagined.

Ultimately the hope is that this work in makeshift spaces in proximity with people's daily lives will be part of a larger shift, in society and in the meanings of "art" and "community"; that our projects will create both fleeting utopias and lasting reverberations. This belief that one can change the world through art collides, of course, with that drop-in-the-bucket awareness of inadequacy.

Complementary colors

I often find myself uncomfortable with the word "tension" itself, because some of the elements commonly labeled as "tensions" are so integral to the fabric of the work that another kind of language might help better to understand them. The idea of "complementary colors" might better express the availability and unavoidability of these corresponding forces that exist in our kind of art-making. What is pleasing about this image is that it implies a palette: the possibility of both mixing and placing side by side, making choices, messes and mistakes, and leaving a stain.

To start with that familiar pair, *process* and *product*, I increasingly understand these as things that are not just held in balance, but intertwined; at their best they are indistinguishable, as in the memorable words of Paula Jardine, "the making of the event is the event." This does not imply a disregard for the notion of "quality," but rather a

Fabric square with passenger pigeon motif

stretching of qualitative caring to all stages, and an extension of the notion of "good art" to include attentive and "good" art-making.

A related pair is *virtuosity* and *participation*: the involvement of expert artists and the valuing of the arts as specialized skills and talents, along with an invitation for everyone to come and the implied message that everyone can in some sense "be an artist." My work with Jumblies deliberately places both of these perspectives within the same container. It is, in fact, one of the defining qualities of the company's work, as well as one of the most enjoyable and challenging things to play with, stretch, test, and explore. The key to success in this respect resides largely in finding (or inventing) combined modes of expression that suit the participants of a particular community—whether they be fabric art, basketball, oral poetry, or spiced tea-making.

Loree Lawrence identifies another very interesting and potentially tension-generating pair: *preservation* and *transformation*. Since Jumblies' catalyst partner on this project is a museum, and one of the project's themes is how memory is or isn't preserved and displayed, questions of "telling old stories, introducing new stories and shifting and broadening the conversation within and across communities cultural and otherwise" (Loree Lawrence) are central to this artistic journey.

Two other terms often viewed as dichotomous are *ethics* and *aesthetics*. Here I feel that the term "tension," theoretical or practical, is misplaced. Without doubt, there are ongoing aesthetic and ethical matters to negotiate, and these can often feel like conflicting urges. For example the desire to make something look "polished" might lead to neglecting someone with less accomplished skills, or conversely the sense of obligation to include an inept participant might lead to an aesthetic result that one finds unsatisfactory.

For example, our props-maker was very frustrated by the mess a group of children made when trying to make *papier mache* tea pots, and ended up repairing and finishing them off in private with another artist. Such common predicaments for us as artists occur, however, as we struggle with the realities of the work and our own limitations. What saves us is an understanding that ethics and aesthetics are friends sitting together on the same side of the chasm from which the precarious bridge stretches; or perhaps they themselves are the substance of the bridge.

As we artists meet each new situation, our imaginations must rise to the occasion with a suitably idiosyn-

> I see the art of hospitality as a great way of integrating virtuosity and participation.
> —*Leah Houston*

> One may, for example, use murals to reassert a past historical moment of a community, rather than reflect the present and ever-changing make-up of the same community.
> —*Loree Lawrence*

Papier maché tea pot, 2007

the tale of her great-grandmother: in fact, the life story of Hawa Jibril from her origins as a camel-herding nomadic girl, through her role in the struggle for Somali independence, to her flight from civil war to a "lonely tower" in Toronto.

Hand dancing

The broader tensions not surprisingly also play out in the project's everyday dealings and details. The overall lack of adequate arts space leads to situations such as a church afterschool program suddenly deciding to use the basement auditorium at the same time as our already established youth workshops and just as we move into our more intensive production period. Lack of a dedicated sewing space threatens to affect not only the quality of costumes we can produce but also the number of people who can enjoy working on them. The need of many groups to have their interests recognized leads to people feeling jealous and suspicious: why, for example, isn't Jumblies running a program specifically for children? Or offering summer opportunities for youth? Why aren't we running any activities at other equally needy local sites? Why are we serving only Somali and not British tea? Or only tea and not coffee? As our Jumblies team strives to resolve these matters, others arise and escalate as the production intensity mounts, until we must accept that this negotiation of momentous or petty details, this taking people's hands as we totter across our tense and fragile bridge, is as integral to the work as is painting the set or rehearsing a scene.

A modest example of adapting aesthetics to include people comes from our regular seniors' workshops. As many of the seniors had limited mobility, choreographer Penny Couchie introduced the idea of "hand dancing."

cratic form of expression: something that can reach its "best" aesthetic outcome in this case and no other. Art has always required trying out things new and chancy—often things that hadn't previously been considered a "art" at all—in order to express and respect what is felt to be important. "Good" art, thus, is "good" ethics, and the creative tension lies between striving for both. It is through being artists to the best of our abilities, emboldened by our talents and specialized training, that we can serve, respond to, and express the communities with which we engage. To go further: through not striving fully on an aesthetic level, we place ourselves in an unethical position in relation to these people and communities from whom we are asking so much.

Bridge of One Hair, our theater piece, was anchored by the words of two poets: Hawa Jibril, a well-known Somali poet living at Mabelle, and Duke Redbird, a Toronto-based poet of Ojibwa descent. The play begins with the two sisters of "Mollie Whuppie," Nettie and Nelly, sending out a reward notice for "the bravest girl in the world." Instead of their own sister appearing, they are overwhelmed by a cacophony of would-be heroes hoping to claim the reward. On of these is a little girl bringing

> Keeping people in the loop, and making sure we're heard, is part of our art and part of our process.
> —*Noah Kenneally*

Faduma Ahmed Alim, Eli Howard, Hawa Jibril and Sirad Yusuf Mohamoud, 2007

The dancing hands were photographed by Deborah Barndt and used as slide projections in the performance, with many seniors in the audience.

Softening of boundaries

There are a number of particular activities that have been developed, invented, and/or borrowed for this project, for example, the personal mapping and the "Where I'm From" poems. However, perhaps the most useful thing we can pass on is the blurring or removal of boundaries: between art and hospitality, creativity and daily life, process and event. This is something our company is learning, and it may ultimately affect the nature of our artistic outcomes in terms of defining and producing something called theater. One of the most gratifying things we did last year was produce an afternoon tea event at the Mabelle seniors building, using place mats and tea cosies made with the participants, mixing cultures of tea (Somali and English) in relative harmony, and offering the event as a gift to the people who had been so generous with their time and creativity. It was a staged and flexible event (control and abandon), art and social goals were indistinguishable, and I, the lover of large-scale highly produced creations, exclaimed, "This is all we need. This is art enough."

Falling off the bridge of one hair

The tea event described here was an "ah hah" moment. Another was the realization, after our June 2006 work-

One of the best practices I can identify in the community arts movement is a creation of gift economies. By this I mean donations of space, people's donations of time and supplies and the gift of their stories and thoughts. When you look seriously at how community arts projects are powered (while holding the gift paradigm in your mind) you see that it is not only the arts councils, nor the funders, but the gifts of people at every level that makes these things go.

—Leah Houston

Fadumah Nkruma singing with projected images by Deborah Barndt

in-progress event, that, despite the fact that many people loved it, others felt disgruntled and unmoved. To this I had two responses: the first a desire to pay greater attention next time to helping people feel included, and the second a conclusion that "you can't please everyone!" and that ultimately I must follow in good faith my own instincts and inclinations, trusting that some, if not all, will like it.

Old woman, I know who you are.

I know this barren wasteland on which I stand was once a forest

And you, old woman, had life and beauty, energy and passion,

Love in abundance, freedom and chatter with the gods.

Birch trees cried, "Here, take my bark, that you might sleep in my arms"

And the great creatures of the forest dropped their fur clothing and said,

> My major "ah hah" moment came one evening with the youth. We'd been talking for months among ourselves and other groups about the themes, narratives and poetic elements of the larger project in general and the "play" in particular. In the middle of a conversation, the teens started asking what the heck we were talking about. I couldn't believe it. In trying to work with so many groups and incorporate so many ideas, while trying to knit together our communications, we'd definitely dropped a few stitches. —*Noah Kenneally*

> When I realized that members of the wider, affluent community were discouraged that the project didn't include their (often told) stories, I also realized that we don't have the resources (or desire) to please everyone. —*Loree Lawrence*

"Let my warmth be your warmth. Make a pillow for your head."

And birds swooped down and laid their finest plumage at your feet . . .

—Duke Redbird, Toronto-based Aboriginal poet[3]

A question that has been unfolding throughout this project concerns the mixing of different artistic traditions. This is particularly marked in the realm of music, but present also in the other disciplines (dance, visual, and poetic forms). Bridge of One Hair attempts to fuse Western composer-led music with Somali conventions of sung poetry, Irish traditional tunes and Caribbean improvisatory drumming. It is surprising that so far this has worked at all, and that most parties are comfortable with the process and results. In our work-in-progress presentation in 2006, the composer did find the Somali singing too extensive, while the Somali singer desired more leeway to add traditional drumming and dance to her singing. The musical director was particularly aware of these challenges as well as their philosophical and aesthetic implications, and

Helah Cooper performs scene with shadow puppets, 2007

> How brave it is of us to try to spin delicate bridges across vast gulfs of understanding, which in essence is what the Bridge of One Hair project is about. Reaching across those gulfs to people for whom following herds of camels and goats across the land was a regular part of life—or to people who've lived in the same town as their ancestors for hundreds of years, only to uproot themselves and come to a place so different and new—or to people who live next door to each other who might never have spoken before. To braid those different strands of stories that we all carry with us into a strong tightrope to balance across those chasms of variety. To attempt to do all these things by making good art together—making something beautiful and vigorous and demanding and vibrant. The idea is so radical, so courageous and creative it boggles the mind. It is so important to encourage people to think of art as a necessary and dynamic part of everyday life.   —*Noah Kenneally*

it is something that we continue to explore as the project proceeds toward full production

Early on a dewy morning

I set off with our camels for grazing

Loping and lolling they led me into the desert

There they were attacked by swarms of flies

And crazed by bites broke into a fiendish gallop

At the heat of noon I herded them into a secluded grove

I rolled a long twine and twisted it around Sigad's teat

So busy was I that I forgot my own food and comfort

In this state I set out on the sunset journey

Yet, because a hungry calf had suckled Sigad dry

Everyone, female and male, bombarded me with blame

Some, offspring of lynxes, feasted on my flesh

Others, howling hyenas, hurled me with curses

But no more, dear father, will I endure this wretched life

—*Hawa Jibril, 1933*
(translation by Faduma Ahmed Alim)

The artists have their own cultural backgrounds to contribute. I draw inspiration from European "high arts," Jewish and British cultures, as well as other sources, including popular theater, folk tales, songs and dances, and international puppetry/visual theater traditions. This is what I have to offer, but what happens when we start to blend traditions and create hybrid forms? What happens when you both hold onto and let go of your own artistic center? The Bridge of One Hair project has stretched me and us more than any other: partly because of the

Joy Douglas and Wanda Krane as Netty and Nellie, 2006

location, and more, I think, because we and the city are ready for this to happen. I was very conscious early on of letting go and how scary this felt, scary because I might just be washed away forever. Realizing this was an unavoidable risk was one "ah hah!" instance. Another was, later on, realizing that I was still floating in the midst of an ongoing change, and that, if I got washed away, it might not be so bad after all.

This returns us to our initial definition of "tension" as the stretched wire or hair or medium between two separated things. A balancing act introduces the possibility of falling, and the place one falls into, the chasm or waters or rapids below, mixes together the two sides. Is it so bad to fall? My experience of this work has shifted from the sensation of tottering on a wire to that of floating precariously in rocking waters. In other words, we have fallen in already and everything is mixed together.

What does "tension" mean from here? How do we talk about it?

This, in fact, is the central theme of the script I have shaped for the project. I am entirely aware of the part of myself that is like our main characters, Nettie and Nelly: trying to block out the clamoring world and clinging on to their own story and obsessive customs. The play ends with them being invaded, disrupted, and changed, but still themselves: Nellie goes off on adventures, and Netty opens up her tea room as a refuge for passing travelers, heroes, and orphans. For us, as the production time approaches, who knows what will happen next; even whether the show will ever really transpire, given that it requires inducing large numbers of Mabelle residents to get on school buses for several days in a row to go to Harbourfront Centre—a place most of them haven't even heard of, to perform in a show, when most of them have

Final bow, "Bridge of Hair" at Harbourfront Centre, 2007

This past Wednesday, as I headed over to Mabelle in the pouring rain, a sense of gloom seeped through my insides. I entered the building at Mabelle and headed down to the basement auditorium. The doors opened and I stepped into the tunnel. The tunnel leads to the auditorium. The floor in the tunnel is a medium grey and the walls are a light hospital blue. Someone has painted a very neat tiny strip of color all along the walls forming a mini rainbow path. When I got to the end of the tunnel, I opened the door and out popped the most amazing scene. There were tables of four set up all facing the door. Everyone was sitting sipping tea, chatting, giggling, surrounded by beautiful cloth and small squares of fabric with little sewn-in designs and beads. The colors were amazing. People were saying to me, "Join us for tea," and Leah jumped up and poured me a cup. I realized that we were somewhere in Wonderland. Soon everyone scurried about forming their own little groups, discussing the project, clearing up and resetting for the rehearsal. Out of the darkness there came light. Out of the tunnel there came tea!

—*Catherine Campbell*

no idea what that means? So yes, abandon and control is at the heart of it all.

Postscripts

June 2007: I am now rereading this chapter from the vantage point of the completed production and the end of a three-year process. The first time our rented bus arrived at Harbourfront Centre full of Mabelle residents, my eyes filled with tears. When people entered the constructed theater area, which we had been approximating in the rehearsal hall and with a scale model for several months, there was an audible sense of pleasure and homecoming. Afterward, several people admitted to having embarked on that first bus without knowing where it was taking them or why. Some had no idea that we were going to "do the same thing more than once," or even that we were going to perform at all what they had been rehearsing for the past ten weeks. Our lack of common terms went beyond challenges of translations. And yet about seventy community members, give or take quite a few, came along for ten days, and were joined in close to equal numbers by performers, backstage helpers, singers, professional musicians, and theater professionals. As always, the production and performance period was an ordeal that some could not endure. It was also a glorious time: an oasis of vitality, joy and social connection that few things can deliver as well as a community play.

Could you see what I see?

Water forming shining pools

Soft winds fluttering our flag

Crops grow and trees show their buds

Now those who from the flames of war

Scattered overseas

Come home alive.

Water forming shining pools

Soft winds fluttering our flag

Crops grow and trees show their buds

Now those who from the flames of war

Scattered overseas

Come home alive.

—*Hawa Jibril*[4]

July 2008: And yet another year has passed. In the fall of 2007, our artistic team wrote on pebbles our desires for the project's continuity or closure, making a path to follow into the next year. Leah, Noah, and others took charge of new ventures: Lantern Garden, summer arts in a Mabelle parkette; Pigeon Creek, a huge pageant at the local school, The Path Project, an environmental installation; weekly sewing, skills-sharing, and food; Somali music and dance gatherings and more. Local partnerships were strengthened with, for example, Madbakh, a grassroots Somali women's agency and Arts Etobicoke, a local arts service organization. People from different backgrounds, who before passed each other as wary strangers, are spied chatting to each other in local streets and apartment lobbies. Bridge of One Hair wins a Great Grants award from the Toronto Community Foundation. Impressed by its success, Toronto Community Housing, offers money to publish a book of poetry by Hawa Jibril, with English translations by her daughter, Faduma Ahmed Alim—launched and celebrated this June by all the people who took part in the play. Now, entering its fifth year, the project has a new name, MABELLEarts, a new young artistic director, Leah Houston, and new plans, collaborators, and funds. People come back to help and take part. New people join in. Mixing art and life is clearly a good idea. Meanwhile Jumblies is planning a new multiyear residency in Scarborough—as far east in the city as Mabelle is west. As we leave, we take along many questions, difficulties, and contradictions, and much persistent, substantiated, and foolish hope.

> And in twenty years they all came back,
>
> In twenty years or more . . .
>
> And everyone said, "If we only live,
>
> We too will go to sea in a sieve,
>
> To the hills of the Chankly Bore!
>
> —From "The Jumblies," by Edward Lear [5]

We take pride in our culture. To see our culture portrayed makes me cry. We always hope for the best, even in the difficult times. I like how many different people and different vocations are involved in the project. It's one of the biggest successes. Our people see how things can be done. They learn from this play structure. And now my mother is known and respected in the building and the community. Since we worked in the local school, the children even recognize her in the street.

> —*Faduma Ahmed Alim* (daughter of Hawa Jibril)

My children participate—this is very good, because my children make friends, learn to be independent and confident. . . . I learn how to use the sewing machine.

> —*Fadwa Jibril* (costume assistant, mother of two participants, and immigrant from Jordan)

I loved all of it—the rehearsal and the show. It was so fun and exciting to work with everyone. The show was my first experience acting and it gave me an idea of the future.

> —*Ala Jibril* (thirteen-year-old Mabelle participant)

CHAPTER 4

TELLING OUR STORIES

Training Artists to Engage with Communities

Christine McKenzie
Catalyst Centre, Toronto, Canada

I t still holds true today that Toronto is "the Meeting Place," as the First Peoples[1] named it. Today, migration caused by capitalist globalization and civil wars makes Toronto a place where people originating from all corners of the world come together. Five million people call Toronto home, 43 percent of whom identify as a visible minority.[2] Of that number, about 30 percent of the population is youth.[3] This dynamic of migration and displacement creates both a diverse society, as celebrated through multiculturalism, as well as its shadow side of oppressions such as racism and classism. When oppression is turned inward, people experience this emotion as depression, hopelessness, or lack of self-worth.

Toronto has been a meeting place for me as well. A place where I was born, a place I have come to appreciate in new ways as I meet people who teach me along the path, and as I learn about myself through these encounters. There are many stories told that celebrate the diversity of Toronto. However, many stories are not told, because they fall outside the accepted image of multiculturalism that obscures racialized oppression. Applying a popular education approach, my colleagues and I at the Catalyst Centre sought to challenge this through an arts practice that collectively and critically examines these everyday experiences, with a political vision that acts in the interests of those who are marginalized.[4]

The Catalyst Centre, a Toronto-based popular education center founded in 1999, spearheaded this vision.

Monument to Chinese immigrants who built the railway.

Our mission is to "celebrate and promote innovative learning, popular education, research and community development to advance positive social change."[5] In working with communities on collective processes to analyze and envision social change, we use popular and community arts to promote multiple forms of expression and to reclaim local voices.

Even though Toronto is portrayed as an urban center where arts and culture blossom, the official stories told do not always reveal the diversity of perspectives of the people who live here. We chose to collaborate with artist educators who work with underrepresented communities, due to the systemic racism and discrimination that creates a lack of opportunities within the arts communities and broader society. In this project we offered a popular education training and analysis, to complement the tool kit of arts education approaches these artists already work with.

And so, Telling Our Stories took root, as a project of cultural reclamation and of art for social change. This took place with the awareness that storytelling is complex; depending on who requests the telling of a story and how the audience interprets a story, we can also run the risk of reproducing the dynamics of oppression.[6] With this vision and awareness, and the generous support of the Laidlaw Foundation and the Ontario Arts Council, the Catalyst Centre joined with artists from across many communities to share, learn, and question the role that art can play in community building and change.

Learning from one another

Through a targeted call for submissions, we chose eight artist educators, based on their ability to represent a diversity of production mediums (dance, song, spoken word, and theater), their desire to pursue arts education / community arts / popular education, and their membership in underserved or underresourced communities (such as people of color, those using unique artistic approaches). These artist educators came together to support one another in making art for social change and to learn and share tools they could use with youth to facilitate arts education workshops. We offered workshops for the eight artists, and then each of them carried out a community arts project with young people.

We consciously put together a diverse team to enable this deep sharing, which produced a rewarding cross-fertilization of skills. As one of the project coordinators I brought my experience of facilitating collective radio production to engage communities in critical dialogues about social issues; I've also used arts and popular education in capacity-building workshops in both Canada and Nicaragua. jin huh and I worked together to make this project happen. She is a singer/musician in an all-female Asian spoken-word band, Maewon, and a writer with both SistahFire, a queer woman of color writers collective and the Korean Canadian Women's Anthology project.

The artist educators in the project brought a huge wealth of talent and insight. Saidah Baba Talibah is a soul/alternative/experimental musician; Mireya Escalante, a Cuban percussionist and singer, founded the Cuban Percussion School and New Cuban Generation group; Lady Noyz, aka Nylda Gallardo-Lopez, is a break / hip hop dancer and choreographer who founded the Drunken Monkz crew, which promotes and educates about hip hop culture and the empowerment of urban youth; Rose Kazi is a singer/songwriter and activist, as well as a member of the band LAL; Shannon Kitchings is an actor and a member of the colored girls' collective; Pasha McKenley, also a member of the colored girls' collective, is a comedy and theater artist and producer; Darren O'Donnell is a playwright and the creative codirector of Mammalian Diving Reflex Theatre Company; Theology 3, aka Theo Steryannis, is a hip hop musician who worked with Regent Park Focus and 4 Unity Productions, youth media arts association, in the Parkdale neighborhood of Toronto. These artists represented a vast array of skills, backgrounds, and communities within Toronto, making the project a rich exchange among all of us.

The process

The First Moment: The Train-the-Trainer Workshop

This collaborative train-the-trainer process brought us together for a three-day workshop to share the art forms and processes that we use when engaging communities, and to learn popular education approaches to add to the artist educators' existing tool kit of educational techniques. We began with ourselves, introducing who was in the room and where we came from, both personally and artistically. Artist educators did this by performing a piece that illustrated the journey that had brought them to the project.

Then we located our work and ourselves in the context of the history of art and social justice. We did this collectively by creating a timeline of art and social justice work, including personal, community, and national/international events, as well as people and ideas that have inspired art and social justice. As we did this, we also reflected on the art and art education processes that helped develop our own critical awareness. As part of our exchange, we shared examples of energizers and icebreakers we use as facilitators to build a sense of community and trust in a group.

Elephants and Giraffes Energizer

1. Everyone stands or sits in a circle with one person in the center.

2. The facilitator explains that the caller is to point to a person at random and yell "elephant" or "giraffe."

3. When a person is called an "elephant" they must raise their arms together in front of their face as if they were the trunk of an elephant and the two people to either side must put both their hands against the ears of the "elephant" to mimic elephant ears.

4. When a person is called a "giraffe" they must raise their arms together over their head as if they were the neck of a giraffe and the two people to either side must both bend down and touch the ground as if they were the legs of a giraffe.

5. If someone makes a mistake (e.g., forgets to bend down), they become the new person in the middle.

6. This game is best played fast with the calling moving from one person to the next quickly and surprisingly.

Busses Icebreaker

1. Explain to the group that you are all at a very chaotic bus station where busses have different destinations than what you are used to. The facilitator will call out the bus destination (category) and everyone is to quickly self-organize to "get on the bus that matches their destination."

2. Start with a simple category that everyone is likely to share and be comfortable with such as "how you traveled here today" or the number of siblings in your family.

3. Once the facilitator has called out the category, everyone must find those people in the group who match their choice and form a small group (e.g., for how you traveled here today, all the people that took the bus must find each other, all the people that rode their bike must find each other, and so on).

4. Once the chaos has settled, groups can spend a minute to learn one another's names and why they are in that group.

5. Then the facilitator can call for attention and do a go-around to ask what exactly the groups are. You can also take a moment and ask participants to introduce themselves to the whole group.

6. Examples of bus destinations: number of languages spoken, community you work with, country (or continent or province/state) of birth, decade of birth, number of children, birth order in your family, number of years with the organization you're with, and so forth.

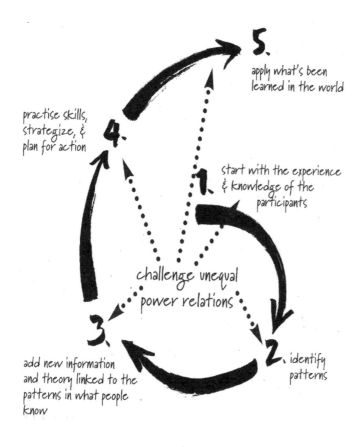

5. apply what's been learned in the world

4. practise skills, strategize, & plan for action

1. start with the experience & knowledge of the participants

challenge unequal power relations

2. identify patterns

3. add new information and theory linked to the patterns in what people know

The spiral model of popular education

We then moved into deeper conversation in small groups, sharing the struggles we confront in doing arts education for social change and the insights we've gained from these struggles. Finally, the artists worked in pairs to plan their community work projects. This was an opportunity for the artist educators to apply the popular education methodology they learned in the workshop and collaborate with another artist to share and combine arts mediums. The process and products generated from these projects would become the focus for the final stage of Telling Our Stories, which was the community performance.

The cross-fertilization, and the ideas generated were amazing! The final stage of the workshop involved sharing the new ideas generated for the community work project. Some proposals brought together different art forms and traditions, as well as means of engaging diverse audiences, some of which we tried together. For example, Pasha and

Shannon led us in a drawing activity and then asked us to create sounds to go with the drawings, producing a collective soundscape to express our feelings, first individually and then collectively. It was powerful to see how the strengths of the group members came together.

The workshop design modeled the spiral model of popular education: starting with participants' experience, identifying patterns in our practices, adding new information or theory, strategizing and planning for action, and finally applying what we have learned.[7] It's interesting to consider some of the links between this spiral—reflecting a dialectical methodology—and the spiral developed to reframe the VIVA! project. Both honor dynamic processes that are grounded in peoples' stories and move toward collective action.

The Second Moment: Artist Educators in Communities

The most important learning, of course, emerged from the projects that the artist educators developed with youth in diverse communities all around Toronto. These facilitators can best describe the myriad projects.

Nylda and Mireya: Hip Cuban Hop, or Percussion Breaking Project

The objective was to create a safe environment for the young women to express themselves through dance, and have a forum to discuss how they feel about the challenges they face as young women in today's society. We began with a historical breakdown of hip hop culture, and a timeline of how music has affected their lives. We discussed the place of women in hip hop culture historically and today, and examined many stereotypes of women in general and in the music industry. I challenged their views (many of which have been instilled in them by the media) by teaching them foundational moves from break dance. This showed they had been underestimating their capabilities and they could do things they had originally considered for men only. Through dance and education it became an empowering and enjoyable experience for all of us. This was different from the work I've already done in the community because I incorporated a self-evaluation piece. By doing that, it allowed the youth to see the correlation between the music that they love and their role in society.

—*Nylda*

After researching about Hip Hop culture I joined with Nylda to develop more ideas about how Cuban percussion is related to hip hop socially and politically, as a form of resistance. We created the Hip Cuban Hop, or Percussion Breaking project. We joined these art forms together and worked with children and youth from ten to eighteen years old at the Oakwood Library Center for the Arts in Toronto. Mario del Monte, who works with me as a partner at the Cuban Percussion School, created beats that could match with the music and the movements of the dancers.

—*Mireya*

The two facilitators made their own discoveries through this process.

I was pleased that many of the young women involved in our hip hop / Cuban percussion project were more aware of the gender discrimination and misogyny in our society than my generation. Relating their struggle to a dance form and culture they already identified with was extremely productive. I had originally thought that the girls would be disinterested in the historical value and theory behind the culture, but they were thirsty for something with roots. It especially resonated with the girls of mixed race background, who could see modern art forms as their own. As a whole, they all seemed to take pride in doing something healthy (physically and mentally), positive and empowering.

—*Nylda*

Nylda Gallardo-Lopez aka Lady Noyz, breakdancing

Cuban percussion school practicing

I learned about another culture, and although I have always been a hip hop lover, I did not realize how related it is to our Cuban culture. It is amazing how much of a culture you can learn through the music; it is a great learning tool.

—*Mireya*

The girls in our workshops learned about Cuban and hip hop cultures, and how they are related. Technically, they learned hip hop dance foundations, which included safe stretching routines, movement basics, strength training techniques, and flexibility enhancement. In theory, they learned about the origins of hip hop (break) dance, and its influences. They discovered the correlation of Black and Hispanic cultures with hip hop and the expression of urban youth for more than thirty years now. Most importantly they came to see that it was their culture to embrace and promote, and that there is a place for them in this male-dominated art form or field.

It definitely increased their self-confidence, as one participant recalled, "Two ladies stopped me after our performance and said, 'never let anyone say you can't do it, because you might get told you can't do it because you are a woman of color, but you *can* do it!' . . . That meant a lot!" Another young participant said, "I learned that I'm not a shy person, that I'm not shy to perform onstage. I am proud of myself because I never thought I could do anything like this. I also realized that people do care about us, and they are willing to come and watch us perform. I want to go on writing songs. My songs are based on young people and what we go through. In the future I want to perform my songs, so people will know how we feel, and how we are not different just because we are young . . . we still can love, we still care about what is wrong."

—*Nylda and Mireya*

Mireya Escalante, Cuban percussionist and singer

Shannon Kitchings, coloUred girls collective

Shannon and Pasha: Script Writing for Youth of Color

Our project was a theater workshop for youth of color between the ages of twelve and eighteen, through two community centers in downtown Toronto. We helped students write monologues based on their personal stories, and offered them tools on directing, acting, and stage management. The workshop was broken down into several components. We first focused on voice, text, and movement, and then used this experience as the material for a short writing workshop. In small groups the youth shared their work and turned this writing into a script that was performed.

Many themes were about youth culture and the challenges of being a youth.

As artist educators we learned how to set up a room beforehand to create a safe and fun environment; and the energizers were a big help and kept the program "fresh" for the kids. We also realized how much the individuals in the group made up the whole. We had some really strong leaders and were able to encourage them to work with the others. It became clear that group effort is a key to success in any program!

The youth in our theater project learned how to work collectively, and to recognize that all stories are individual and unique even if drawn from the same inspiration. They also learned how to breathe, to project their voices, to use different forms of theater, to write and incorporate music and movement into their pieces, and to connect to an audience in different ways.

—*Shannon and Pasha*

Theo: Telling Our Stories through Film Production

Our project took the form of a short film produced and directed by two youth from the Parkdale neighborhood in west Toronto. The film content was entirely scripted by the youth and related to issues of self-empowerment, respecting diversity, and reaching for personal goals. My role as a facilitator was to provide technical assistance with editing and filming, to manifest a safe and comfortable space for creative interaction and to help the script writing process by encouraging fluidity in the storytelling.

The youth involved had very interesting stories to tell in relation to their personal journeys and family situations. I encouraged them to explore some of those feelings without limiting their imaginations and the result was a fantastic film screened at the final community event. This short film showed clips of the communities where they live, and gave them a chance to speak about why they are proud of where they come from.

Some of the things I learned from this experience were vital for my future youth engagement projects. By creating a safe and welcoming space where new ideas are welcomed, youth opened up and felt no limitations in their expressions. Some of the icebreakers that Christine and jin utilized during our sessions were very effective with the youth, I was pleased at the level of trust and sharing that we had during the writing, filming, and editing process. It was a great experience.

The youth learned that they can affect the message by controlling the medium. Many of the stereotypes that they felt were unjustly placed on them were combated through the film. They felt empowered by the whole process of gaining a collective voice.

The most important thing that happened for me personally was seeing how two different art forms came together in this project to expose the common link, and to see that all art shares a common link. It is about being part of a whole process of finding that, and seeing how art can affect kids who aren't necessarily trained in art, but are developing as people. . . . This [project] showed me that art by its nature is political, and watching it in this way shows the empowerment of people, which is the core of social justice."

—*Theo*

Darren: Beach Balls 41 + All

I facilitated a donation of four hundred inflatable pool toys from a local grocery store to Alexandra Park pool's Wacky Fun Day. The intention was to induce an encounter between two sets of people who have very little contact. This was between the artsy culture types of Toronto and the kids who frequent the pool; they usually come from Kensington Market, the Alexandra Park Housing Co-op, and surrounding area, which are comprised of a variety of ethnicities with lower than average household incomes. Getting these two groups together for a moment was motivated by a desire to create a small alliance between the two populations, to offer the adults an opportunity to act in the interest of the kids, and to have the kids be beneficiaries of fairly random, spontaneous generosity. The intention was not so much about reversing an already existing power dynamic—though it did do that—but rather, introducing a relatively new and different dynamic, if only for the duration of the day.

An unexpected result of the event was that adults and children who did not know each other played together, breaking one of the most sacred rules of childhood. The prohibition against talking—let alone playing—with strangers is irrational; children are more likely to be molested or abused in the safety of their own home than by any playful adult on the street. It feels odd to try to advance the idea that children benefit from

Come together at Beach Balls +41 event

playing with strange adults, not because the idea is particularly outlandish, but because it isn't outlandish at all. The whole thing looks to be a case of notions of security and safety once again cloaking social control.

No matter how powerful the individual, when you're only wearing a swimsuit and are up to your neck in water, you've got to go with the flow—almost everybody becomes a kid again and all parties have the potential to benefit from experiencing the effects of this equality. Play holds abundant possibilities for public intervention and interaction.

More generally, through the Telling Our Stories project, I learned a lot about working in com-

munities, the obstacles and intricacies of trying to navigate the flow of a community, the priorities of a community center, and the work of an arts education project. I spent a lot of time trying to work my particular art practice into the community arts and arts education framework and found it quite challenging since my art breaks with many conventions.

—Darren

The Third Moment: Celebrating Our Time Together in a Community Performance

Once the community work was completed, all artist educators and community participants came together to perform at a community event. It was a magical event, with all performances warmly received by close to one hundred audience members. For the majority of youth this was their first opportunity to perform publicly and they were energized by the experience. They left with a feeling of pride in their accomplishment, a hope in connecting across differences and passion to continue the work they had begun. We heard this from audience members and participants alike as they aired their views in front of a video camera at a "speaker's corner" at the event, among them these evaluative comments (which can be heard on the video accompanying this chapter):

> It was very interesting, seeing different ideas from different communities coming in.... I learned that they can mix very well together.
>
> I think art is a very effective way to get the point across because a lot of people don't listen to activists, and a lot of people don't listen to cultural music, so when you bring them together it is very powerful.

Tensions emerging

While there were many moments of insight and celebration, the unanswered questions provide the greatest insight, leaving us pondering as we continue to act. In fact, if questions are so easily answered or production processes neatly packaged, it leaves me wondering what may have been overlooked. Through questioning both ourselves and our practice, and the role that art plays in society, we surfaced several tensions which we continue to wrestle with.

The Role and Value of Political Art in Society

The value of political art in society is a complex issue and one very close to home. All the participating artist educators make their living from a career in art, while at the same time facilitating arts education within various communities on a voluntary basis. Throughout the train-the-trainer workshop with the artist educators, this tension was expressed in several ways. Participants reflected that, for the most part, the public, participants, and foundations greatly appreciate the use of art to convey social justice messages. However, this is rarely expressed or compensated in monetary terms. This surfaces a ten-

sion in terms of what value art, particularly political art, has in the mainstream culture. Is art's value beyond or outside the monetary, or is this merely a means of discounting its worth and limiting the scope of creation and commentary?

In the train-the-trainer workshop, Theo, aka Theology 3, shared how he navigates this dynamic in his work with budding hip hop artists and works to empower them to stand behind their message before looking for exposure. In this piece, Theo expounds on how art is used to continue dynamics of oppression within a racist capitalist economy. Here he addresses how hip hop artists need to be proud of claiming their art form, as opposed to diminishing its value and playing shows for free. He also comments on how artists need to stand together in solidarity, instead of turning on one another within the competitive environment of the music industry.

> Time
>
> I need to remind you, don't waste your time giving power
>
> to those who can't sign you
>
> It's time to stop giving debts if you ain't friends
>
> Stop killing MCs, start killing main men
>
> It's time to recognize Toronto's greatness,
>
> but understand down deep Toronto's racist
>
> It's time for you to retire
>
> Time to stop making money off of putting black faces on flyers
>
> With no black presence at your jam on your street team
>
> Time to stop doing shows just to be seen . . .
>
> It's time for me to take control
>
> Time to break the mould
>
> Time to wake your soul
>
> It's time
>
> —*Theology 3*

A second tension emerging in the project speaks to the partnership of political vision and art. Darren points to situations where it is an awkward addition to bring art(ists) within political coalitions when their political analysis may not be "up to speed."[8] While there is an important role for artists to play, it is not a given that their contribution will be politically strategic or savvy. This was true as well in Telling Our Stories projects, where participants' analysis did not always make the connections between personal and systemic change. While developing our analysis is part of the journey, we need to think critically about what spaces this journey should best take place in. Art and arts processes do not automatically further political causes or transformative change.

Emulating Pop Culture vs. Finding One's Own Voice

This tension directly links to the previous discussion of the role and value of (political) art in society. In creating art within the capitalist context, there are certain hegemonic[9] ideals that are held up for artists to aspire to. This bleeds into every area of identity, style, sound, and message that the artist conveys. In a climate where the motivation for many is to become famous, how does finding one's own voice figure in the process? How can we use art, and inspire others to use art, to explore diversity in all its aspects without falling into (or seeking) homogeneity?

This was a tension in creating art with youth, who are searching for themselves while at the same time emulating pop heroes. Making political art in this context is a challenge when there are few role models to lead the way. In this respect, artist educators in the Telling Our Stories project had an important role to play in inspiring the vision of their participants.

We recognized that while art can facilitate consciousness-raising—allowing others to share their views as in the experience of the women's movement—this could be a challenging venture. There is an ongoing need to remain vigilant and strong in approaching art and popular education not only at the cognitive rational level but also at the emotional and feeling level, despite the external and internal opposition we may face.

Final reflections

As a group of facilitators and arts educators, we analyzed all the practices that had been shared in the project during a collective debriefing session. At this time two themes emerged as the most crucial to doing this work in a way that touched the minds, hearts, and souls of those who participated.

First, we found it is important to explore new ways to engage communities through collective artistic production processes and to overcome key obstacles. We recognized a barrier that can exist within many budding artists, and even within ourselves. We often judge ourselves by some external measure of what "an artist" is supposed to be, or be able to do. This prevents us from expressing what we have to say to the world through our own creative processes, because we silence ourselves. Peer support and affirmation is crucial to overcoming this!

Secondly, we affirmed the importance of creating processes that meld art and social justice. In a context where much social conflict remains beneath the surface and unacknowledged, we need to be able to talk about racism, violence, and personal empowerment. We found that expressing diverse and silenced identities through song, dance, writing, or other art forms is a powerful way to name these issues and confront these barriers.

Going forward

While the formal phase of the Telling Our Stories project has concluded, the connections and the experiences live on in the work the artist educators continue to do with communities. For example, Theo and Saidah are now collaborating on a screen writing workshop process for youth. It is exciting to see this process of ongoing collaboration and community support in a context where artist educators and the youth participants alike noted a lack of any similar space or process of this nature that brings together and trains progressive artist educators, and artists of color in particular. We look forward to navigating a path into the future to create and sustain spaces that engage in diverse art forms while raising critical questions about culture and art.

CHAPTER 5

A Melting Pot Where Diverse Lives Converge

Tianguis Cultural de Guadalajara

Leonardo David de Anda Gonzalez and Sergio Eduardo Martínez Mayoral
Tianguis Cultural and IMDEC, Guadalajara, Mexico

Please come in: be our special guest.

The plaza is calling.

There are no isolated policies or actions, only collective initiatives, developed by trial and error. The team members of this unique independent action are facing a challenge and its resolution depends on us. Our public is ambitious and eager to learn, young, enthusiastic, and curious.

Cultural activism is a journey made by walking. The greatest sign of strength of Tianguis Cultural rests with this community: the city's youth who claim their place in society and are willing to fight for it.

Good citizens, you who are committed to the yet unresolved social causes; you who are part of communities struggling between a conservative society—whose false moral values disguise intolerance, racism, and prudishness— and innovative values that aim to build a kind, inclusive, sensitive urban space.

In the midst of the contradictions we experience within Tianguis Cultural, our greatest contribution to the city would be to keep this space alive, as a melting pot where lives converge and where hope is fostered.

For us the VIVA! project represents a hopeful and important initiative. It is encouraging and heartening to connect with similar projects across this continent that share our critical perspective, promoting artistic and cultural practices that challenge and question the dominant systems of power. This openness toward new forms of knowledge and practice must continue.

It is an honor to participate in and contribute to this kind of biography that tells the unofficial story of our America; the paths we are forging help ensure its future by putting into practice new and dynamic forms of organization. Such initiatives will generate concrete results and provide a fruitful scenario that reinforces ethical, aesthetic, and political values guiding us on our life's journey—on both our individual paths and our journey together. For us, life is a process of spectacular blossoming, of eternal springs aiming for peace and harmony. Here's to life!

The birth of Tianguis: Creating a space for youth

In December of 1995, we formed a group called Tianguis Cultural de Guadalajara (Cultural Marketplace of Guadalajara), and created a cultural gathering place, a kind of market of music, art, and ideas, as a way to encourage the creation and spread of alternative urban and popular culture. Every Saturday we set up an alternative market in a public plaza in Guadalajara, the second largest city in Mexico. Legally established in 1998, our project promotes self-employment through the sale of diverse yet original products, basically cultural in nature. This exchange shapes and stimulates life-affirming urban identities. As one of our members noted, Tianguis helps people not only to pursue a livelihood but also at a deeper level to see themselves as youth with alternative visions, as people who can act and shape their world.

Tianguis Cultural in Juarez Square, Guadalajara on a Saturday

Since its origin, Tianguis Cultural was envisioned as a space for recreation, community building, making connections, and creating popular culture, involving the young people who live in the metropolitan area of Guadalajara. Yet Tianguis brings together different generations of people as well who find affirmation, enjoyment, and inspiration in the cultural activities and the marketplace itself.

The Tianguis project has created a public space for rock bands, Latin American musical groups, painters, photographers, performers, poets, dancers, and so forth, who gather in the central square to share their creative work. The reputation of Tianguis is built on its uniqueness as the only public space that, for twelve years, has maintained a forum of discussion and creative urban culture.

The *tianguis* (from the Náhuatl language *tianquiztli*) was a market of the inhabitants of Mesoamerican towns, set up during particular periods, where merchants coming from nearby towns gathered together to offer their products. The legacy of the *tianguis* is a combination of the different commercial traditions typical of pre-Hispanic towns, including the Aztecs and the Middle-Eastern bazaars brought to America via Spain. The *tianguis* with the greatest tradition are normally very colorful, as both the blankets used to protect the stands from the sun, and the flowers, fruits, and spices are of rich vibrant hues. Paintings by Mexican artists such as Diego Rivera or Rufino Tamayo depict these scenes in all their vivid color. It is also common that the *tianguis* are frequented by traditional musical bands, so they are a lively example of traditional Mexican culture.

Our motivation

The historic student movements and grassroots organizing from the 1980s laid the groundwork for Tianguis.

Sergio Eduardo (Lalo) Martínez Mayoral (center) with other drummers

During that period, some of us were involved in diverse underground expressions of resistance in the cities and on the streets. These took on a critical, antiestablishment role of denouncing and protesting the perceived discriminatory and repressive nature of society, particularly in Guadalajara, known as a very conservative city.

The founders of Tianguis Cultural come out of that generation of urban organizers and share that rich history. Whether engaged in rock performances on the street or selling handicrafts, books, and magazines, they helped consolidate these kinds of spaces for young people, validating the role of youth within their own communities.

This motivation persists today, supporting young people, embracing their diversity and their problems, working to combat drug addiction, promoting a responsible sexuality, giving youth access to public spaces, and encouraging them to defend their own urban youth culture and aesthetics.

The history of our space

At present, the Tianguis Cultural is set up every week in the Juárez Square, situated between two major boulevards in downtown Guadalajara. The site is especially meaningful because it was once the site of a lake known as Agua Azul, or Blue Water. Through the colonial period and until the middle of the twentieth century, it was used regularly for family leisure activities. In the mid-1900s, this area was "modernized," becoming the site of various public institutions: the Archaeology Museum and the Handicrafts Museum, an outdoor band shell, two theaters, the public library, as well as the government TV station headquarters and the Jalisco Cultural Center. In effect, ever since Tianguis Cultural was set up, this site has recovered some of its former meaning and greatness, with an array of diverse events taking place there.

After the four founders (Leonardo David de Anda, Olga Rivera, Sergio Fong, and Alejandro Zapa) developed its organizational structure, chose its name, and designed its logo, Tianguis Cultural opened for the first time in late 1995 in the historical center of the city. This was after months of negotiations with reluctant municipal authorities.

Between 1995 and 1998 the number of Tianguis exhibitors showing their creative work grew from eighteen to two hundred. As the market expanded, certain neighbors, business people, and the local church authority expressed displeasure with this youth-run marketplace. The noise from the crowds and problematic behavior by some visitors to the market fed an intolerance that was also fed by the media. The negative publicity associated with countercultural youth came to be known as the "black legend" of the Tianguis.

In 1998 Tianguis Cultural was incorporated, and its structures formalized. We created an organizational council and divided among members a variety of tasks such as design, promotion, logistics, audio systems, and administrative duties. That same year, the city council of Guadalajara attempted to relocate Tianguis to a park, eight blocks away. This action brought Tianguis Cultural into the public eye. We organized a press conference to denounce the move and stimulate public expressions of protest. This helped legitimize our purpose and reinforced Tianguis's roots in the community as well as its urban, political, and social identity. Nonetheless, conservative groups and the media continued to push the city to go ahead with the move; and when it was aborted, there was even greater hostility from the city council.

As one of Tianguis's founders, David de Anda was arrested along with five members in a raid-like operation on what appeared to be a peaceful Saturday, until tear gas and beatings interrupted the calm. Many of the exhibitors and visitors led a march to the municipal police offices to protest these arrests resulting in the six members' immediate release, without charges. Eventually, however, by the end of 1998, Tianguis relocated to its original and present site.

What happens in Tianguis Cultural?

For over 700 Saturdays and for more than a decade, we have offered musical events, dance, theater, puppets, *capoeira*, martial arts, drummers, mime artists, and more to approximately ten thousand visitors who support our work every week. We also have a cultural center open to the public throughout the week for diverse activities such as meetings, exhibitions, presentations, and workshops.

We aim to make our organization democratic and transparent. Elected council members and officers are responsible for putting the decisions of the membership into practice and for ensuring the quality and effectiveness of our main activities, which include an alternative marketplace, cultural fora and activities, audiovisual and print media, as well as performances.

The alternative marketplace

Having a cultural marketplace that emphasizes cultural not commercial values has encouraged tremendous growth in the number of exhibitors at Tianguis Cultural (currently 350). You can find a great variety of products: books and handicrafts, musical instruments and records, handmade clothes and accessories. The commercialization of imported products or the selling of pirated products is prohibited, while the local production of cultural goods is protected.

Cultural activities

Every Saturday we feature a local or national rock band and, occasionally, a band from another country. Latin American musical groups, popular musicians, and new singers also perform. We have presented theater and puppet performers, as well as popular and modern dance ensembles. Visual arts exhibits and bulletin boards are also regularly on display.

Booth for weavers and jewelry makers at Saturday marketplace

We organize specific annual activities, such as A Day for Peace, The Festival for Humankind, and The Altar for the Dead. Sometimes as part of Cultural Week, we take Tianguis Cultural to universities and secondary schools in Guadalajara and other cities. Ecology Day is another notable event, offering an educational component, as well as activities such as fence painting, planter repair, lawn mowing, and tree planting.

Discussion and training

Many activist organizations are members of Tianguis, promoting ongoing discussion of many different issues

left: Mixtec artisan carving a gourd

of concern to young people. Publications on diverse subjects—history, health, poetry—are regularly distributed. Our community work also includes the Young Liberators, a cultural campaign that involves presenting some of the most powerful artistic expressions from Tianguis in other venues.

Through audiovisual and printed media as well as promotion on the radio, we are recovering and reintroducing cultural practices that have been lost, such as songs and unique types of artistic expression like the *palomazos* and the *batucadas* (a type of Brazilian samba). Giving new life to these traditional forms of art awakens the interest of students, professionals, and journalists, who are encouraged to tap these sources of creativity and use them in their work. These efforts have been well received by market-goers and exhibitors alike.

All who attend are inspired in some way by the broad range of events offered at Tianguis: from the social change proposals and actions sponsored by social movements to an African dance or a ceremonial Huichol song; from a sax solo or a ska band to the, contagious rhythms that make everybody dance the slam. The energy of cultural expression merges with a deep social commitment and nourishes other kinds of coalitional actions among the groups in events outside of Tianguis itself.

The multicultural dynamics of Tianguis

A wide range of people bring Tianguis to life, from exhibitors and performers to market-goers and residents. Our job is to help facilitate communication between them. Most market-goers are younger than thirty, but there are also seniors, families with children, middle-aged teachers, and professionals.

The approximately 350 exhibitors include NGOs, Indigenous groups (Huicholes, Mixtecos, Zapotecos, and Indigenous groups from the state of Chiapas), individual artisans, craftspeople, painters, collectors, antique dealers, music distributors, booksellers, and ecologists. The young exhibitors may be high school students or university students, primarily studying the humanities, arts, and cultural promotion. Others specialize in craft-making trades. This universe of exhibitors tends to be educated, sensitive, environmentalist, committed, critical, friendly, and supportive. Unfortunately, there are also a few who are driven mainly by commercial interests, who infiltrate the marketplace and take advantage of the many benefits derived from its immense popularity.

Many local cultures converge at Tianguis, including subcultures who adopt ideologies from other places and social movements. This diversity can be seen in the mix

Artist in the tattooing and body piercing area of the market

of groups often found at the market: anarchist groups, punks or anarchist-punks with libertarian and emancipatory politics; acid rock fans, ravers and electronics, who prefer electronic, psychedelic, trance and techno music; skateboarders, rollerbladers and extreme cyclists who, depending on their mode of transport, can be seen jumping over ramps, spinning through pipes, sliding down banisters and performing all sort of extreme antics. Rock fans, neo hippies, musicians, and drummers also attend; there are the gothic enthusiasts, the itinerant artists with their tattooed and pierced bodies, the banda kids, the posh, philosophers, poets and writers; artists, mime performers, theater devotees, university students and professionals; teachers, geniuses, and eccentrics, all gathered together within a single area. The market creates a space for this diverse universe of people to coexist and interact in a healthy way. No matter what their dress or style they can express themselves in all their amazing difference, and share their worlds and ideas without being criticized or belittled.

Amid the jumble of shapes and colors, you might see a Rastafarian, with tangled dreadlocks, wearing vivid Jamaican garb, exchanging music and information with an

top left: *Eulalia Zavala, Wixarika artisan and healer*

bottom left: *Alfredo Ruvalcaba, Gothic urban artist*

Social movement activists in NGO and social activism zone

exuberant punk showing off a mohawk or spiky hairdo, loaded with studs and chains hanging from his coat and patches with slogans sewed on his pants. You might find a young stylish teenager, concerned about the latest fashions, taking pictures of herself with her cell phone camera while posing beside an artist who has metal everywhere on his face and who has just pierced the girl's belly button with an eye-catching piece of jewelry. This is the scene every Saturday. This rich diversity brings vitality to a community space where people are entitled to freely express their concerns about social change and renewal in ways that respect their differences, build solidarity, and provide them with opportunities to question and transform the oppressive nature of their society.

The ongoing struggle for public space

During the administration of the conservative mayor Fernando Gaza (2001–2003), we once again found ourselves under attack. The authorities wanted to break off the agreements made with Tianguis Cultural and to impose a costly regulatory system. The Tianguis directorate of the municipal city council, which regulates all markets, has tried to open up Tianguis Cultural to merchandise that has no affinity with our cultural project, such as imported goods and products that don't reflect our values.[1]

In defense of our original purposes, we protested and organized public demonstrations. Adopting a strategy

Juggler performing in cultural marketplace

of resistance, we have been able to avoid closure of Tianguis, especially since the election of a new municipal administration that has been more supportive of our work.

In the midst of contradictions

Operating in a public square strengthens our civic effort to promote cultural diversity but, at the same time, operating as a market subjects us to city regulations and to the will of politicians in power. This dynamic has shaped our history and given rise to a seemingly fundamental contradiction. Throughout twelve years under the administration of four right-wing municipal presidents, our identity and our very existence have been attacked. Officials have tried to belittle and delegitimize our work by trying to turn our alternative cultural marketplace into a purely commercial market. How can we demand our right to organize an independent cultural gathering space and organization and, at the same time, make use of a public square? This contradiction remains unresolved, perhaps because politicians feel threatened by our independence and the potential within Tianguis to promote real social change.

Yet we carry on in the face of these challenges. For example, tension exists around the question of professional or volunteer staffing and support. Members of our organizational council receive no remuneration for their altruistic and voluntary work while people who carry out certain logistical tasks do get paid. While volunteer involvement reflects a deep commitment, it also presents inevitable problems such as the lack of completion of tasks, tardiness, carelessness, and resignations that undermine the project. Coupled with this, there has been suspicion about irregularities in the financial management of the project, adding to the overall problem.

Internal power dynamics within Tianguis

Our annual meeting involves the participation of the associated exhibitors, administrative council members, founders, and other contributors to the project. They elect executive officers and representatives for each area who report regularly about their activities. In return for active participation in the decision-making and carrying out specific duties, they receive a space in the market or forum where they can present their handicrafts, organize their cultural activities, or present their ideas.

Although a democratic process is emerging within the organizational structure and among the leadership, one of the founders still has inordinate influence in determining the policies of Tianguis. In contrast, the participation of women in leadership positions is weak and needs to be addressed.

Our internal process is shaped by the lives and problems of our members, whose participation is limited in part because their economic circumstances are often precarious, their support work is not remunerated, or they lack a strong personal commitment. It is an extremely complex issue, since two of the founders dedicate enormous effort to the collective project, negotiating with government authorities, while the authorities try to discredit and delegitimize them, by accusing them of authoritarianism and manipulation. Internally,

the management policies are based on decisions taken by the membership promoting a horizontal organization. Despite the lack of remuneration, we need our leaders to assume their full responsibilities and act in ways that help resolve problems where personal envy and resentment prevail.

How does Tianguis challenge the dominant models?

Tianguis Cultural is neither a political party nor a union. Nor is it simply a marketplace. Tianguis Cultural is a courageous citizens' initiative that has been able to connect a universe of ideas, proposals, and diverse ways of seeing the world: it is a living space that nourishes the very dynamism of our city.

The main concern of those in power is that an effort like Tianguis Cultural may become the site of activities aimed at subverting the establishment such as antiwar marches, actions in defense of sexual diversity, or demonstrations against the government repression in Atenco or Oaxaca.

The unique synergy generated by the gathering of diverse groups through Tianguis epitomizes the emergence of a new generation that seeks political and social changes, as well as a new kind of relationship with the Earth. Tianguis Cultural is part of a broader movement that is more and more relevant over time. Tianguis is an institution, a human complex that gathers artists, performers, and activists of different and even contrasting creeds, political inclinations, and lifestyles. The principles of Tianguis endorse that diversity. In our opinion, it would be a mistake if we decided to become a faction or a party, since that would be in conflict with our policy of being inclusive. A more partisan exclusive approach would offend many of our visitors and supporters.

Tianguis Cultural, then, remains a political project, based on explicit philosophical principles. It is inspired by the historical countercultural youth movements of the 1960s and 1970s. During that time, countless aesthetic and political expressions emerged to challenge the culture of patriarchy and authoritarian power. A new category of youth and a new age emerged—promoting a new form of horizontality in human relationships calling for the transformation of dominant culture and the implementation of new policies that gave greater freedom

Three generations of batik artists

to public and private spaces. It was at this inspiring time when social movements were born and flourished—ecological movements such as Greenpeace, the civil rights movements in the United States, the Chicano movement as well as movements such as feminism and lesbian / gay rights. This time was no mere "romantic" or "utopian" moment, but on the contrary, it transformed contemporary global culture; it laid the foundation for today's movement of antiglobalization activists, the defenders of urban identities, and supporters of Aboriginal movements. These leaders and activists are developing new transformative and more participatory forms of leadership and organizations inspired by visions of ecological stewardship and solidarity. They are putting into practice new ways of doing politics. The way in which organizations (including Tianguis Cultural) position themselves as movements capable of effecting transformative change is still uncertain. Currently, we are made up of minority, marginal, and even underground movements, facing our own internal challenges within our own organizations.

The challenges we face

The problems facing Tianguis threaten to overshadow its principles and objectives as a promoter of diverse cultural events. Operating as a market involves Tianguis in the neoliberal economy's worst dynamics, where one individual's financial success is often at the expense of another's. In fact, a number of exhibitors have been evicted for not adhering to our cultural principles. Not only did they betray the project by commercializing their work, but they have adopted attitudes that, ironically, serve the interests of the conservative authorities.

According to our policies, any violent behavior entailing extortion, illegal sale and rental of spaces, or explicitly commercial activity should be penalized. People who undermine Tianguis Cultural's reputation justify their dissent by affirming that "the only authority is the municipal government." At the present time, over 300 exhibitors out of a total of 350, participate fully in the Tianguis's cultural forum and adhere to our principles. We try to resolve conflicts institutionally, promoting active membership, and encouraging a sense of unity. This is part of a process of education and consciousness-raising that will ensure the survival of Tianguis Cultural.

We have long-term goals for our work, which include the founding of a production cooperative based on the experience of the market's craftspeople and artists and the identification of new commercial markets to support these products. We also hope to create a free university that will build on members' talents and potential through participatory research and collective knowledge generation. The university's main purpose will be to help individuals develop critical thinking skills and strategies, to analyze and question authoritarian neoliberal policies and the destructive consequences of their enormous power for our culture.

The development of alternative media is also considered strategic, since it would help raise the visibility of the diverse voices present in Tianguis. This communication strategy requires a type of professionalism that we are still lacking but are actively seeking through partnerships with experienced groups (such as the VIVA! project members) as well as with other nongovernmental organizations like IMDEC,[2] with its expertise on popular communication. It is of utmost importance and urgency that leftist movements in our country respond to this challenge given that mass media outlets are increasingly being taken over by corporate interests and their power concentrated in fewer and fewer hands. Alternative perspectives disappear as corporate messages and perspectives dominate the airways and brainwash every household through television. In response, we hope to challenge this trend and actually try to create an alternative TV channel aimed at serving the interests of the community.

Tianguis and its message of hope

Once again, in late 2006, the city council of Guadalajara voted to dismantle Tianguis as an alternative forum for urban and popular culture. This decision bans us as a civic organization and prohibits us from organizing cultural events. At this moment, Tianguis Cultural's fate may seem hopeless, because this ongoing struggle wears us down.

Yet, the fact is that Tianguis Cultural is still here, calling all who will join us to continue this collective, multidisciplinary, honest, and versatile initiative. The obstacles and threats are real, but these ups and downs call for cooperation, channeling such wonderful collective energy to keep the project alive.

PART III

Community-University Collaborations

Blurring the Boundaries

Introduction

Just as the global cities featured in the last section reveal the erosion of the nation-state and thus make geopolitical borders less relevant, so, too, are universities rethinking the conventional borders between universities and communities. There are several trends in North America toward greater collaboration in the new millennium, among them service learning, co-op education, funding for collaborative research, and knowledge mobilization. Service learning encourages students to volunteer with organizations and institutions outside of academia as a form of experiential learning for academic credit, while co-op education places students in workplaces to gain employment experience as well as credit. In the Canadian context, community-based research is becoming more legitimized within academia[1] and new federal funding programs have encouraged collaborative research,[2] while universities such as York University have set up Knowledge Mobilization units to nurture community-university collaborations as well as to popularize research results in forms that speak to a broader public. Popular education and community arts, in fact, have a lot to contribute to these efforts to bring research and education out of the ivory tower, and to acknowledge and promote community-based knowledge production processes that can contribute to a richer and more socially useful understanding of the world around us.

The VIVA! project itself reflects the emerging trend toward blurring the boundaries between universities and communities. Collaboration was a key principle at two levels at least: locally as partner organizations collaborated with both universities and community groups, and transnationally, as

Muralists Antonio, Checo Valdez, and Pancho in La Culebra, Chiapas, 2005

we met annually to share the results of locally grounded participatory action research across our distinct contexts. Both Latin American university partners, UAM-Xochimilco in Mexico and URACCAN in Nicaragua, were founded as community-engaged universities: UAM has maintained a close relationship with Indigenous communities in the southern Mexican state of Chiapas, while URACCAN decentralized its operation to nurture the regional autonomy movement. A third university-based project, the ArtsBridge program at the University of California, Los Angeles, represents a collaboration between the School of Art and Architecture and the urban public schools in poor inner-city communities.

These initiatives have not been devoid of contradictions, however, especially as they have collided with other troubling trends within the neoliberal university: greater dependence on private and corporate funding for research; a prioritizing of science, technology, and business over the humanities, arts, and social sciences in the allocation of state funds; a market-driven curriculum that assumes the university's main purpose is to secure well-paying jobs rather than nurture the development of critical thinking and active citizenship. The projects discussed in the next three chapters are all

sites of resistance to these trends within the university, while also having to contend with them.

Sergio G. (Checo) Valdez Ruvalcaba, a professor in social communications at UAM-Xochimilco, became part of that university's community-engaged research and education in Indigenous communities in Chiapas, within the context of the autonomous communities of the Zapatistas in the late 1990s. In fact, he developed his participatory approach to community mural production modeled after the Zapatista mantra *mandar obediciendo* or "leading by obeying," referring to a vision of leadership as taking direction from the people. In his chapter, "Painting by Listening: Participatory Community Mural Production," Valdez reflects on two of the many collaborative mural projects he has undertaken, one in an urban context with the School of Anthropology in Mexico City, and the other with Taniperla, a rural community in Chiapas. In the latter case, the mural celebrated the declaration of autonomy by the community, and provoked a military attack on the eve of its inauguration, landing Valdez in prison for a year along with local Zapatista leaders. While this may appear to be an extreme consequence of collaborative and socially committed work, it does reveal the fact that community partners are often taking greater risks and that even community arts can be threatening in repressive contexts. In this case, Valdez was able to summon solidarity actions from groups around the world, who reproduced the mural in their own cities; years later he was also able to develop a university diploma program in community mural production that built on those collaborative international relationships.

In "Connecting the Dots: Linking Schools and Universities through the Arts," Amy Shimshon-Santo clearly grounds us in the global city of Los Angeles, acknowledging that the dynamics of neoliberal free trade have increased migration from the South, resulting in greater numbers of undocumented Latin Americans. These could even be the same people (or connected to them) that Checo Valdez works with in southern Mexico to represent their history, as the poorer Indigenous populations have lost access to the land as private multinational interests have bought it up. Shimshon-Santo also reveals how these global inequities are reproduced both within Los Angeles public schools (in terms of resources) and within the University of California, Los Angeles, where the ArtsBridge program is housed. Her efforts to place university arts students in inner-city schools has opened up new opportunities for both the high school students as well as the arts education students. She addresses head on the question of how art projects in the schools can contribute to community development and to political change. With examples ranging from legislative theater fighting for the rights of undocumented students to dance educating the public around health services, ArtsBridge blurs the school/community boundary as well. The multiple forms of artistic practice brought into classrooms are healing and empowering, challenging the domination of text-based knowing and affirming the notion of multiple intelligences and other ways of knowing.

The University of the Autonomous Regions of the Nicaraguan Caribbean Coast (URACCAN) was founded as part of the autonomy movement of the historically marginalized Atlantic coastal region of Nicaragua. Thus its mission as a bilingual intercultural university was always grounded in local communities, with multiple small campuses spread throughout the region. The project that Margarita Antonio and Reyna Armida Duarte describe in their chapter, "With Our Images, Voices, and Cultures: BilwiVision—A Community Television Channel," exemplifies the potential role of universities to provide the tools for community members to recover their own histories, identify the issues of concern for them, and make their multiple and multilingual voices heard. This is participatory action research with a camera, and the transformation of television programming from foreign dominated to locally controlled.

There is another kind of collaboration referred to in this final chapter. As is often the case of universities outside the orbit of the west, urban centers in the third world, and the academic mainstream, URACCAN has depended on funding from international development agencies, charitable organizations, and northern universities. In fact, York University was contracted by the Canadian International Development Agency (CIDA) to offer graduate training to URACCAN's new professoriate; I was part of the York team that was sent to the coast in 2000 to offer a course in Popular Intercultural Education while over twenty URACCAN instructors came to Canada to study for their master's degrees at the York University campus in Toronto.

Such university-to-university collaboration is also being promoted as part of an intensifying internationalization of the neoliberal university,[3] which does not always honor local knowledges. In fact, just as university-community collaboration is becoming more recognized as academically legitimate and supported with substantial funding, it is being critiqued for perpetuating the structural inequities upon which it is often built. An in-depth study of collaborative research projects in British Columbia, Canada, concluded that while there was more money available for university-community partnerships, there was less for community groups to do their own research, in fact they were being pressured into such collaborations. And in most cases, the research agendas and methodologies were predominantly determined by the university partners, perpetuating deeply seated inequities.[4]

As with all other critical reflections on the VIVA! projects, we have to continually ask of the collaborative relationships: who is benefiting and in what ways?

CHAPTER 6

PAINTING BY LISTENING

Participatory Community Mural Production

Sergio G. (Checo) Valdez Ruvalcaba
Metropolitan Autonomous University (UAM-Xochimilco), Mexico

W hen I was heading toward Taniperla in Chiapas State in southern Mexico to facilitate the mural workshop, it occurred to me that maybe they were expecting me to paint the mural, while it was my intention that *they* would conceptualize and paint the mural. So I began to ask myself: how am I going to tell them that I am not going to be painting, but rather they are? On the day after my arrival, I had an interview with the local authority, who gave me the official welcome, told me who would be participating in the community work, and assured me that everything was ready to start the project. Before I could even start to tell him about my concern, he exclaimed, "Oh! But don't think *you're* going to be painting, you're only going to be our adviser!" I was truly charmed; it was a real meeting of minds.

This is the story of the birth of a project of participatory community mural production, entitled "Painting by Listening." But first, let me offer you some context for understanding why it was born and how it unfolded.

An immense and diverse country

Mexico is a country of great contradictions, opportunities, inequalities, and social unrest, operating within the confines of a capitalist economy. Despite its dependent and underdeveloped nature, the country's economy possesses enormous wealth. Yet these riches have been plundered by national and international forces for centuries and further undermined in recent decades by free trade policies.

Comandantes David and Javier in front of mural of Zapata, Oventic, Chiapas, 2001

Mexico comprises a vast territory spanning almost two million square kilometers.[1] Its topography is diverse, with a great variety of climates, ecosystems, and a complex geological, geographical, and biological history, including enormous biological diversity. Mexico is one of the twelve countries in the world categorized as mega-diverse.[2]

Mexico has a population of over 105 million people, half of whom live in poverty, and one-third of whom experience hunger and acute poverty.[3] About twelve out of one hundred Mexicans belong to one of the sixty or more native ethnic groups still present in the country, and about ten out of one hundred Mexicans are white. Most of us are mestizos coming from a wide variety of mixtures as a result of colonization, migration, and movements of exiles; Mexico is, in effect, a country of many countries. Its population is a multicultural kaleidoscope that originated from three great branches: Indigenous, European, and African backgrounds.[4]

The inequalities embedded in the Mexican social fabric have been challenged historically, most notably during the Mexican revolution of 1910, and most recently, with the uprising of the Zapatistas in 1994, at the moment of implementation of the North American Free Trade Agreement (NAFTA). The Zapatistas have spawned a new grassroots movement led by Indigenous peasants for the most part, centered primarily in the southern state of Chiapas.

A community-oriented university

In the year 2000 the country had 812 universities, 324 of them public and 488 private. Among the more prestigious universities is the Metropolitan Autonomous University-Xochimilco (UAM-X), where I work. An institution such as the UAM-X offers opportunities that are as unexpected as they are original. Such is the case of our project of participatory community mural production, which is part of the Social Communications Department.

The interaction and relationship between the UAM-X and its social environment is a central feature that runs through the university's main activities: research, teaching, and service—activities that are not implemented in a linear and isolated fashion, but rather simultaneously and integrated with each other.[5] Although the university facilities are located in Mexico City, we undertake activities throughout different regions of the country and abroad. In 1998, a group of professors from the arts and communications department went on a field trip to Taniperla, an Ocosingo municipality in the state of Chiapas, at the invitation of Professor Antonio Paoli, director of the project Tzeltal Culture: Education and Values.

This visit gave birth to a new project focused on community mural production. The initial idea was to produce a *gran obra*, or "great painting," right there in Taniperla, to celebrate the upcoming inauguration of the autonomous rebel municipality of Ricardo Flores Magón, a Zapatista community. Such a mural project required an educational process to help prepare local people for the challenge. Thus, the Community Mural Production workshop Painting by Listening was born.

Development of the Painting by Listening method

Phase 1: Born within the Zapatista Movement

As we look back on this moment, we can see that it was the impetus for developing a much more comprehensive initiative that has generated enormous creativity and community action over the years not only in Mexico, but beyond. When the authorities of the new municipality asked for our "advice," we agreed that there had to be full community participation. The municipality agreed to contribute 50 percent of the expenses while the rest was to come from individual contributors as well as myself, the project facilitator.

This communal approach meant that community members had to determine the theme of the mural. It was an exceptional opportunity for us to practice participatory and collective methods of teaching creativity in a context of active communal life. It was also a challenge, because the "great painting" of this project was, in fact, to be conceived by community members themselves, from their own perspective, and by people without any previous experience in drawing or painting.

Our specific purpose was to create a mural using the ideas and the direct participation of men and women of all ages from the communities in the municipality, making sure that all the different aspects of their lives would be included in the painting. The goal of this experiment was to unveil a mural painted on the wall of the municipality as a part of the official celebration inaugurating the autonomous community.

In initiating this project, we asked ourselves these questions:

- Is it possible that people without previous experience in drawing or painting, working as a team, can produce an artwork that reflects the community?

- Will the involvement of men and women of different ages and communities ensure a more inclusive representation of the community spirit?

- By painting collectively, will important communal values surface, converting the painting into a catalyst for analysis and reflection?

In general, the process consisted of various approaches, both reflective and graphic. These involved directly tapping the ideas of the people involved as well as gathering ideas indirectly through informal surveys of people from the wider communities within the new autonomous municipality. As we were committed to an inclusive strategy, we integrated all ideas, producing a mosaic of topics that ranged from people's origins to their aspirations for the future. Once the group created the final design, we drew a sketch on the recently painted facade of the municipal building called the Common House that was to be a meeting place for the many communities in the area. As we started painting, adding color to the drawing, we were joined spontaneously and enthusiastically by other people

Zapatista Comandantes David and Javier in Oventik, Chiapas, 2001

from the different communities, as well as national and international visitors.

The mural painting *Vida y Sueños de la Cañada del Río Perla*, or "Life and Dreams of the Ravine of the Pearl River," was completed on April 9, 1998, only to be destroyed several hours later by government troops. As the community celebrated their achievement, word was received that police and soldiers were on their way to raid the party, challenging their proclaimed status of political autonomy. Among the many atrocities that occurred that day was the destruction of the community mural. Along with the community leaders, I was imprisoned for one year, but images of the Taniperla mural were reproduced in twelve other countries as a symbol of resistance and solidarity.

Despite these events and the short life span of the mural, we felt that the method we had used in developing the painting had been effective in stimulating the group's artistic expression. So our key ideas were affirmed: that it was possible to tap the talents and potential of ordinary community people to produce murals in their localities that express their identities and social concerns, and that a broader consultation with surrounding communities ensured wider participation and more effectively portrayed the values, feelings, and interests of the municipality.

The next opportunity we had to organize a mural workshop and test the viability of our approach was with inmates of a prison in Tuxtla Gutierrez, Chiapas. The inmates came from another Zapatista municipality, the autonomous rebel municipality of Tierra y Libertad, and declared themselves an autonomous community. To identify themes for this mural in a participatory way, we did a survey among the inmates and their numerous visitors. The resulting mural was framed by the silhouette of a white dove; inside the figure of the bird, the daily activities of people living in the municipality as well as symbols of resistance were portrayed. It was entitled *The Dove of Land and Freedom*.

The inmates participated in the entire process along with their families, friends, and some community groups. The mural was presented as a "visual lecture" at a meeting between civil society groups and the National Liberation Zapatista Army that was held in November 1998 in San Cristóbal de las Casas, Chiapas. This second experience further underscored the effectiveness of the approach and deepened our understanding of the method.

Phase 2: From Rural to Urban Contexts

In the early 2000s, we began the mural production process in Mexico City at the National School of Anthropology (ENAH). This project emerged from an initiative by a group called La Tribu (The Tribe) in response to the occupation of their school by the federal police. At the time, the police were repressing the student movement in the National Autonomous University of Mexico (UNAM) and had occupied the School of Anthropology as a "preventative measure." This project represented a radical change in the kind of social group we would be working with as well as in the type of context. Our arena of action went from a rural to an urban environment, from an Indigenous culture to the culture of the university. That context made us rethink our conceptual approaches and theoretical foundations,[6] testing our participatory community mural production (originally conceived in the context of a rural community culture), with social groups belonging to different cultural and geographical contexts. In effect, it made us rethink what we meant by "community," as we tried to identify the shared values of urban groups who might see themselves as a community of identity or interest rather than of geography.

We undertook a systematic inquiry within the academic community, consulting with students, teachers, workers, and administrators of the School of Anthropology. Out of three final proposals emerging from this inquiry, one was selected. An open invitation to join the mural production team brought together mostly students, with some university workers and one professor rounding out the group. Based on the survey with the larger academic community, they produced a mural entitled *Del Lagartijero*, or *From the Lizard's Nest*.

When we propose a collective mural, people immediately take on the mural as their own. Whether they feel connected by geography, gender, or livelihood, they share certain common activities and interests, and consider themselves in some ways a community. This group-building process is begun as they vote to approve the project and is further deepened as people are asked about the specific content they would like to see highlighted in the mural. It is strengthened by including their suggestions of content, and by inviting them to participate in of all the activities; it deepens as different design options are presented for public approval and as

Mural at the National School of Anthropology and History, Mexico City

the painting is finally sketched out and completed on the designated wall.

A very powerful speech made by one of the participants of the project at San Miguel Ajusco reflects on this experience:

> It is the first time we've been asked if we agree to a project, it is the first time somebody asks us what we want, it is the first time we've been brought together to participate and it is the first time we've approved of something beforehand![7]

In a context where paternalism and clientalism (dependence on the state) have reigned, and where artists have usually been professionals and outsiders, community mural production is an empowering and radical act.

The festive and fun part of the process starts when the drawing and painting actually begin. As the sketches take shape on the wall, the community begins to recognize their own ideas and images; more people begin to par-

ticipate in the process and the mural turns into an object of self-reflection. As one of the participants in the mural production in the autonomous municipality of Oventic said:

> The mural shows things as they occur in our daily lives. The mural allows people to judge for themselves whether or not the Zapatista leadership (EZLN) is telling the truth. That is the main purpose of the mural creation.[8]

Phase 3: Expanding to Other Communities

The year 2002 marked a third stage in the evolution of the project with a research project that broadened and expanded the original community mural work into other areas. Entitled Communal Creativity: An Approach to Social Communication, the research aimed to encourage communities to identify their own qualities and needs, as well as their social, spiritual, and political aspirations

"Children of the Corn" mural in Oventik, Chiapas, 2001

by developing community-based artistic expression as a means of social communication. Through this research, we developed fourteen similar projects between 1998 and 2005. Reflecting on these experiences, we came to three important conclusions.

1) A mural, created through a constant dialogue process by a group in a particular community, can become a powerful transformative tool for social communication and solidarity, strengthening the group's recognition of its cultural, social, and political identity. For example, one of the participants at the Oventic project concluded:

> We are Mayan, but another kind of Mayan, not the ancient ones, because the development of their culture was interrupted and undermined by the Spanish colonizers. Now we are resisters, so our right to be both Indigenous and Mexican can finally be recognized.[9]

2) The role of the facilitator of the participatory community mural production is crucial, as she or he must encourage the participation and ideas of the community members and of the core group, while refraining from imposing his or her own ideas on the conceptual weaving of the mural.

3) The forms and colors as well as the visual design must come directly from the participants' ideas; the facilitator creates an environment for listening and for exchanging thoughts and feelings among participants.

While our experiences in community mural production have confirmed that our method was effective, it also revealed that women tend to participate in the mural teams much more than men, something that is common in community arts practices in other countries.

Phase 4: A Diploma in Community Mural Production

Based on these various experiences, we eventually designed a diploma program, through a course in participatory community mural production entitled Painting by Listening. It consists of two main parts: the first in the classroom, followed by practice in the field.

The development of the course marked the beginning of a fourth phase in our mural work, aimed at training people to become facilitators of participatory community murals. It was open to people interested in social, cultural,

Painting the Taniperla mural, La Culebra, Chiapas, 2005

political, educational, anthropological, and sociological issues and who identified with a social group that can be defined as a type of community (both rural and urban). The purpose of the course was to train and enable facilitators to run mural workshops with both skill and flexibility.

Since participants completed the course in August 2005, they have each carried out projects in many different contexts including Chiapas, Veracruz, Mexico City, Sonora, and Chihuahua in Mexico, as well as El Salvador and Munich, Germany.

Reclaiming culture

Through all these experiences of mural production, participants have explored the historical and cultural origins of the group or community, recovering stories and aspects of their identities that had been lost or repressed. In the murals of Taniperla, San Miguel Ajusco, National School of Anthropology, Oventic, San Salvador, San Cristóbal, Tepezintla, and Sierra Maycoba, there are references to a wide range of themes from pre-Columbian, colonial, traditional, modern, as well as futuristic topics. In some, the main theme is culture itself, such as the CCH Vallejo mural focusing on communications media.

In some cases, groups are reclaiming their cultural uniqueness, as reflected in this comment by a participant in the San Miguel Ajusco mural:

> What I would like to know is why I was born here, where the Tepacnecas come from, who I am. I like my community a lot—the countryside, the mountains. And I do not want a McDonald's or a Kentucky Fried Chicken here.[10]

Other common themes include resistance against hegemonic powers and the denouncing of social injustices; murals lend themselves to this kind of message:

> I really like how we express ourselves through the mural, consulting the residents of the neighborhood. Political demonstrations are fine, but a mural lasts longer and is seen by more people.[11]

Still another common theme involves relationships between human groups and their social and natural environments, as well as their hopes for a better world.

Ethical values and communal creations

During the workshop, we aim to help participants develop confidence, solidarity, honesty, hard work, joyful-

Mural produced at VIVA! workshop, York University, 2003

ness, and cooperation through a variety of activities and exercises. These activities are based on ethical values and principles such as listening, respect, and consensus. Listening means putting ourselves in the other person's place; respect means honoring the heart; and consensus means making everyone's ideas our own and making them happen.

The facilitator's ability to put these principles into practice is critical to the approach and it is important that they be shared among the core group. These principles are seen in action throughout the design process as ideas are gathered and compiled from the surveys, as results are fed back to the community, and discussions are held to finalize the plan. Adhering to these principles ensures the use of processes that sustain and nourish the community, as well as a visual design with images that affirm its relationship with its environment, its aspirations, and possibilities for transformation.

Through the community-based mural production process, a core creative group develops into a cohesive team that is built on its members' sensitivity, creativity, knowledge, abilities, learning skills, and generosity. These attributes allow the group to look at itself critically while helping the community to recognize its own worth and dignity, to reclaim its cultural roots, and to reinvent itself.

Community-based and participatory education

The rewarding experience of working together this way reflects the traditions of the original communal cultures of Mexico and is fully congruent with Paulo Freire's pedagogy of the oppressed. We found the principles and practices of participatory research and popular education crucial for stimulating creativity and teamwork.

The key organizer of a community mural project plays many roles during the process—coordinating, encouraging, organizing, teaching, learning, animating, administering, questioning, relating, delegating, intervening, among others. This ability to perform such a multiplicity of roles helps ensure that the specific objectives and goals of the mural production are achieved. It is the skill of a good facilitator to nurture a deliberate process of participation, design, and community art-making.

Working across differences

In our work, we try to understand and relate to people in all their complexity—as human beings who are made up of biological, psychological, sociological, and spiritual dimensions. We work toward affirming these aspects of people's beings as an integrated whole through a variety of exercises and activities that focus on feelings, body aware-

San Miguel Ajusco, Mexico City, 2002

ness, mental exercise, creativity, group interaction, critical thinking, silence, and personal affirmation.

Building relationships across generations in the community begins by inviting men and women of different ages, occupations, preferences, and cultures to participate in the project and to share their ideas, stories, fears, and desires. The process is broadened through surveys done with expanding numbers of the community to determine the themes for the mural.[12]

Intercultural relations are often part of these experiences. For example, there may be a mestizo facilitator working with an Indigenous group or with different ethnicities within the community itself. Sometimes mural projects also involve national and international volunteers, as well as people coming from different neighborhoods and socioeconomic levels. In all of these instances, relations of power must be taken into account.

The first group to take the diploma course reflected this intercultural interaction, with people from Mexico, Chile, Canada, the United States, Germany, as well as people with dual nationalities such as El Salvador and Canada, Mexico and Argentina, Mexico and Peru. Regretfully, due to lack of financial resources and logistical problems, there were no participants from any Indigenous backgrounds in the first course, but since 2007, courses have

been offered in mural-making in Indigenous communities in Chiapas. Whatever the circumstances, our guiding principle is that we work from diversity and we encourage the idea of "being equals among differences."[13]

Our cultural interactions have been broadened through our work with the VIVA! project (since 2004). This relationship has brought formal exchange opportunities with a wider community of colleagues, including two York University graduate students, Heather Hermant as course assistant and Alexander Goss who joined the mural team in the El Kipor project in Sonora, with diploma graduates Rafaella Fontanot and Susana Petersen.

Social tensions, education, and creativity

As the mural process evolves, social tensions can develop that affect people negatively. Most often these tensions arise due to the ambition and domination of a few over the needs and aspirations of other group members. Such attitudes threaten to undermine the process for the wider community and are rooted in what in Zen Buddhism are known as the three great poisons of humanity: greed, hate, and ignorance. These attitudes are also fed by the structural dynamics of neoliberalism and corporate globalization.

We also fight against the homogenization of culture that is part of corporate globalization and that attempts to reshape culture to the preferred size and taste of a dominant middle-class population, for whom national, regional, local, and ethnic cultures are nothing but an obstacle. Because cultural production such as mural-making helps affirm a community's sense of identity and collective power, national and international elites may work to undermine its capacity to mobilize and energize people.

Depending on their own particular circumstances and conditions, communities resist these attacks, using their ideas, organization, commitment, and creativity to defend their lives and culture—their values, knowledge, and relationships with their environment. This resistance is often expressed through festivals, costumes, tools, family relationships, and forms of organization, all based on custom or syncretic practices. Sometimes this resistance is taken up by multiethnic political and social organizations, such as the Congreso Nacional Indígena (CNI, National Indigenous Congress) and rebel organizations such as the Zapatista National Liberation Army.

The forms of resistance are multiple and diverse, but our projects focus particularly on forms in which we are more proactive, such as social communication and artistic production. Strong cultural resistance is found in traditional aesthetic expressions created by ethnic cultures; music, dances, dresses, costumes, painting, crafts, oral tradition, and literature, all belonging to a broad and very complex universe. Though they can be considered forms of cultural resistance, and a source of pride and resilience, they are slowly being eroded due to cultural and economic pressures. Some artistic expressions are undermined or even disappear as a result of interactions with neighboring cultures or with commercial and industrial sectors that can lead to a change in consumer habits.

Within the context of commercial artistic production, social tensions provoke creative responses that take many forms: from anonymous songs with social messages to those by well-known songwriters, from rural theater to legislative theater, from zines (handmade self-published magazines) to electronic web pages, just to mention a few. Participatory community mural production may adopt one of three approaches:

1) for the community—either the amateur or professional artist conceives of and produces a painting for the community;

2) with the community—the painter conceives of and then organizes the production process with community members acting as assistants;

3) from the community—the artist/facilitator promotes the creation of a mural from the community based on their own themes, images, and participation in the design and painting process.

Our participatory community mural production method follows the third approach.

When creating a mural with this kind of participatory method, social tensions can occur through the collaboration. Frequently caused by issues of power and rivalries among authorities and local public employees, some factions may try to control and get credit for the project or someone may deliberately obstruct the activities because they perceive community participation as a potential threat to their own status. In all our experiences to date, these local tensions have been resolved—through the group's persistence and commitment, consultation with the community, public sharing of the results, communal decision-making, and team work.

Group tensions

On a more intimate level, as any person accustomed to group work knows, inevitably there are tensions that emerge within a group. These may be caused by dynamics originating with the facilitation process or by attitudes on the part of the group leader, who in worst case scenarios can be seen as pretentious, authoritarian, rigid, improvised, self-centered, lazy, or dishonest. The resolution of these tensions requires critical self-reflection, proper preparation, and the establishment of clear ground rules for group participation. It is quite rare to find creative solutions coming from the group itself unless a process is developed to encourage their own reflection and action.

How these dynamics and attitudes play out largely depends on the ethical commitment and the emotional balance of each person. They can deepen antagonisms and rivalries as well as forge alliances with oppositional forces. Such negative expressions are harmful, and complicate and distort the project. They usually arise from ignorance and a sense of inferiority or insecurity of people who seek their own status through the denigration and marginalization of others. The diploma graduates did not escape this problem, which means that these kinds of attitudes and

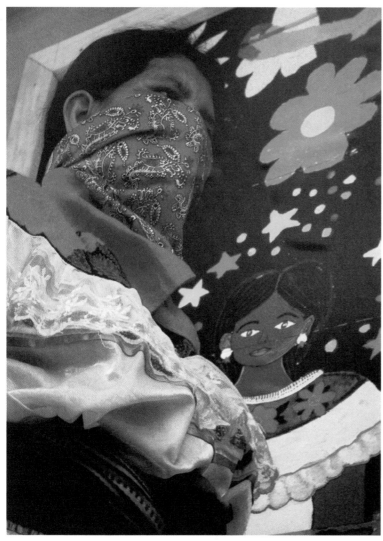

Mariana, model for Taniperla mural, 2005

dynamics need to be addressed in the course and in the mural production processes themselves.

As part nurturer, coordinator, cheerleader, and friendly provocateur, my role as the diploma coordinator was to develop techniques and strategies that would help build a participatory and mutually supportive group. This role also involves creating a climate of shared responsibility where the group itself assumes the challenges of developing the attitudes and skills necessary for accomplishing their transformative goals. These include, for example, generating and focusing energy and commitment, opening up their hearts and minds to personal change, critical thinking and growth, and feeling more comfortable with uncertainty and complexity.

While there are many theoretical and practical resources for developing appropriate content and specific exercises to meet these challenges, they often go untapped. At least one-quarter of the diploma course should be devoted to these activities. Sadly, many facilitators disregard this crucial aspect of learning and personal growth and underestimate its importance. For this reason we emphasized these group activities in the diploma course and suggested them as resources for the participants to use within their own communities or social groups.

Following the end of the five-week diploma course, and while the diploma candidates were undertaking their own mural projects, we organized a series of exchanges between participants to discuss their different field experiences. Once again we affirmed the validity of the methodological, theoretical, and practical approaches used in the mural production. As leaders of community mural processes we realized that we need to improve and broaden our skills as facilitators as well as deepen our theoretical understandings and capacities to more effectively respond to the inevitable challenges presented by future projects.

In addition to community mural production, the methods followed in our diploma program could be adapted to other types of participatory community arts projects such as theater, poetry, dance, painting, video, photography, crafts, and popular communication. The approach could also be adapted to address basic development needs such as health, education, and other services.

Currently we are analyzing the diploma program and the experiences of related mural projects, so that we can more systematically learn from our work, draw conclusions, and provide insights to those interested in community arts in general and community mural production in particular. Perhaps our greatest contribution has been to take seriously the Zapatista mandate *mandar obediciendo* or "lead by obeying," meaning that genuine leaders serve the people and take direction from them. By adapting that slogan to our community mural production process, *pintar obediciendo*, or "painting by listening," we are advocating a broader vision of a leadership and learning that honors the diverse voices and images of people who have been marginalized—from land, economic survival, political participation, racial and gendered structures, and, in the case of the VIVA! project, from ways of expressing their histories and identities in multiple artistic forms.

CHAPTER 7

CONNECTING THE DOTS

Linking Schools and Universities through the Arts

Amy Shimshon-Santo
UCLA ArtsBridge, Los Angeles

Creativity in education has the potential to spark student and teacher learning, help participants identify their personal and community strengths, and affirm cultural and linguistic diversity. Having creative outlets in school is necessary to support the whole child as an intellectual, physical, and emotional being. When viewed in relation to Los Angeles' diversity, access to creative learning opportunities takes on social justice implications. Local struggles for access to arts education are best understood with an awareness of local diversity and geography, as well as broader regional tensions. This chapter identifies positive personal and social change supported through an arts education partnership between a university and public schools in Los Angeles' inner city. While the arts education partnerships offered children instruction in visual art, design / media arts, dance, architecture, music, and drama, this analysis pays particular attention to movement and media studies. Stories from dance education classrooms demonstrate how movement study can support critical thinking, challenge limiting gender stereotypes, and transmit silenced cultural knowledge. In addition, examples from media studies classrooms reveal how incorporating new technologies in arts education can support students' bilingual language and cultural assets while reducing the digital divide.

Watts Towers, or Nuestro Pueblo, built by Sabato Rodia

Building community across geographical and educational borders

Los Angeles' cultural diversity is sometimes framed as a new phenomenon, but nothing could be farther from the truth. Long before Los Angeles became famous for "Hollywood" it was home to the Tongva Nation. Later, in the 1700s, the city was colonized by an intercultural group of Mexican settlers who gave it the elaborate name El pueblo de nuestra señora la reina de los ángeles del rio de porciúncula (The Town of Our Lady the Queen of the Angels on the River Porciuncula). Even back in 1781, the city was home to people of African, Native American, and European descent. In fact, the first city census verified that many residents were a mixture of more than one cultural group, and half of the residents were of African, or part African, descent.[1]

How would you tell someone about your neighborhood if they had never seen it, or had only heard stereotypes about the people or place? Contemporary depictions of Los Angeles have been constructed in the global imagination through television, films, magazines, and lyrics that venerate or denigrate this place and the people who live here. On the ground, Los Angeles is many things to many people—nearly four million people who live in the city proper and approximately ten million who live in the county. While Los Angeles is a recognized center for cultural and artistic production, what many people don't know is that it is also a blatantly unequal place to live. The real disparities here would rival the greatest cinematic production in dramatic force.

The Los Angeles I know feels like an international gathering place since many residents here are connected to distant countries through familial ties. Los Angeles is not easily understood in its entirety—not even for residents who live somewhere in the city's 500-square-mile radius. There is simply too much to see and know, histories are often forgotten or distorted, and many neighborhood stories remain confined to their local contexts.[2]

The ArtsBridge program discussed in this chapter is located at UCLA's School of the Arts and Architecture in Los Angeles. ArtsBridge helps participants create pathways in the arts and higher education by fostering closer contact between public schools and universities. Given the geography of Los Angeles, this is no simple feat. UCLA is bunkered by the affluent neighborhoods of Beverly Hills,

Urban landscape of K–12 schools, Los Angeles

Suburban landscape near UCLA

Bel Air, and Brentwood while the majority of partnership schools were located in South or Central Los Angeles that is framed by a box of divisive freeways.

The first ArtsBridge partnership I cultivated for UCLA Arts was with David Starr Jordan High School in Watts. In the 1900s, Watts was an important transportation nexus nicknamed "the hub of the universe." The Central Avenue jazz district emerged in South Los Angeles contributing to excellence in jazz innovation. South Los Angeles has experienced a long history of struggles that have transformed the racial and ethnic landscape of the region; from First Nations' communities' painful experiences with the Spanish colonizers, to the war between the United States and Mexico, to the institutionalization of restrictive housing covenants and school segregation policies through Jim Crow laws. History is the backdrop for current struggles for educational and social justice. Today, South Los Angeles continues to change and is increasingly populated by Latino families in addition to African American and Pacific Islander households.

Privilege and discrimination were historically engraved into the city's geography through restrictive housing covenants and formal educational policy. The court case *Plessy v. Ferguson* (1896) solidified white privilege in education by declaring racial segregation our national legal precedent. Racial segregation was formally sanctioned in education for sixty years. While the landmark case *Brown v. Board of Education of Topeka* (1954) finally rendered desegregation unconstitutional, the important role Mexican Americans played in challenging school segregation is lesser known. Eight years earlier, the *Mendez v. Westminster* (1946) case found that Mexican American student's Fourteenth Amendment rights were being violated. Mendez was the first successful case to successfully question the constitutionality of segregation.[3] Despite the formal reversal of legal segregation in 1954, over a century after the *Plessy* case, Los Angeles' primary and secondary schools remain segregated by race, ethnicity, and class. The lack of parity in primary and secondary schooling spills over to reproduce further inequalities in higher education that keep the Californian educational system from reaching its democratizing potential.

A host of risk factors from poverty to addiction, from urban violence to a failing foster care system, and from environmental degradation to a lack of rewarding jobs, frame the lives of youth in Los Angeles Unified School District (LAUSD). These larger issues outline the cultural, educational, and geographical context for activism. The extent of Los Angeles' educational disparities are astounding and disheartening to say the least. A simple comparison of student enrollment in LAUSD with UCLA is revealing. While 74 percent of LAUSD students are Latino, only 14 percent of UCLA students are. While 11 percent of LAUSD students are African American, only 3 percent of UCLA students are. LAUSD high schools, by and large, are populated by Latino and African American youth who are struggling to overcome obstacles that classroom teacher Joy Downing explains "make many children in low-income areas feel shut out." In contrast, UCLA is primarily populated by Asian American and white students. Not surprisingly, this exclusionary dynamic is also seen in the lack of faculty diversity that, in turn, negatively impacts campus culture and leadership.

While ArtsBridge is a network of universities whose common goal is to strengthen arts education in underresourced schools in the United States, each program site has some flexibility to implement this common vision. ArtsBridge programming at UCLA began in 1990, but this chapter focuses on the program between 2005–2009 when I served as its program director at UCLA's School of the Arts and Architecture (UCLA Arts).[4] I focused our efforts on increasing rigor in teaching artist preparation at UCLA, improving campus coordination between like-minded service learning and outreach programs, and building community off and on campus to leverage resources for primary and secondary schools. The community-building focus harmonized well with the VIVA! project vision as we worked to cultivate mutually beneficial partnerships between the university and the community in a school district with majority Latin American students and families. We hoped to have a positive impact that transformed both the university and inner-city schools for the better.

At UCLA, ArtsBridge Scholars take preparatory courses in arts education and are recognized for their efforts with academic scholarships to design and facilitate sixteen- to twenty-hour sequential standards-aligned arts education residencies in their genre at a high-needs primary or secondary school. The ArtsBridge Scholars have diverse skills and interests from spoken word to painting, hip hop to Polynesian dance, dramatic arts to architectural design. A facilitated group cohort provides space for creative, intellectual, and professional growth among emerging arts educators. They share their concerns about what it means to be an artist who teaches in urban schools, how this affects their own creative process and life choices, and how to work closely in community to support student learning.

We also facilitated access to on-campus and off-campus cultural resources for youth, classrooms teachers, and administrators. At UCLA, field trips, exhibitions, and performances for youth, teacher-in-service programs for classroom educators, and summer arts institutes for high school students help prepare youth for college in the arts. ArtsBridge also supports connections between local community arts resources and neighborhood schools. Thomas Turner, lead teacher at George Washington Carver Middle School, compared working with ArtsBridge to "growing dendrites," or transmitting nerve synapses, in the body.[5] Mr. Turner's biological metaphor beautifully explains the connections that flourish in a supportive educational ecosystem.

Community-building through arts education supports an interactive environment where sharing and leveraging important resources can flow more easily. Community-building was a crucial immediate transformative aspect of our process. Doing so required that we: 1) get to know each other and our different learning communities, 2) become available and accessible to each other, 3) be honest, diligent, and patient with each other, and 4) take meaningful risks and actions to achieve our mission.

Community-building also required reclaiming and articulating what we care most deeply about. It required aligning our personal visions and skills with community goals and desires. These processes planted the seeds of social change through civic engagement and leadership development at multiple levels within the classroom, household, or neighborhood, and in our different schools and universities.

John Muir Middle School students study design

Personal and social transformation

One might ask, "what constitutes political action and how does arts education connect personal and social change?" The feminist movement, the civil rights movement, and the environmental movement have argued that sexism, racism, and environmental degradation are reproduced through historically constructed political, economic, and social institutions. However, each of these social movements has also recognized that personal action can be political. The reproduction of oppression is undergirded by negative misrepresentations of marginalized people and places. In contrast, the power of self-definition through creative expression allows creators to imagine themselves and the world in more accurate and empowering ways. An education that affirms cultural reclamation sparks personal changes in consciousness that are building blocks for larger social and institutional change.

One example of how participants cross borders between personal and social change is illustrated in a collaboration inspired by a group of students at George Washington Carver Middle School who created a play called *Welcome to the Border Now Go Back Where You Came From*. Their play was developed with teaching artist Lee Sherman of the Center Theater Group in collaboration with humanities teacher Thomas Turner. Techniques from the Brazilian theater activist Augusto Boal's Legislative Theater were used to create a play about im-

migration and educational justice. The students' original play included a powerful tableau with a line of teenagers grasping arms to form an impenetrable wall of bodies that stretched the width of the auditorium. The youth wore block letters strung around their necks that spelled out the word b-o-r-d-e-r. The first time this tableau appeared in the play, it represented the United States-Mexico border. A young actor playing the role of an immigrant called out "Ayúdenme!" (Help me!) as they attempted to pry open the wall and cross over. "Está dificil!" (It's hard to!), the actors forming the wall replied in brash unison, their heads hanging down. In a subsequent scene, the youth resurrected the border tableau again, to represent another border—the border to higher education. First, an actor playing the role of "undocumented student" moved successfully through primary and secondary school with high grades. "Congratulations!" her teachers said, as she received diplomas for excelling at each phase of her studies. But, after high school, the wall reappeared again on stage. "Ayúdenme!" the undocumented student called out as a placard reading "college" was held above the heads of the border tableau. As she tried unsuccessfully to cross the border into higher education the actors yelled back "Está dificil!" while she struggled helplessly.

At the end of the play, the cast welcomed questions and answers from the audience. One classroom teacher asked the ensemble, "Now that you have made a play

George Washington Carver Middle School students perform at UCLA

about immigrant student rights, how will you change legislation for undocumented students?" A perplexing silence ensued. Was it enough to create an educational tool that drew attention to the topic without proposing changes? Clearly not. At this opportune moment I was able to be an open door rather than a barrier to the university. I praised the students for their work and invited the young actors to UCLA to perform their play and to meet with student activists on campus who have been formative in changing legislation for undocumented students through Assembly Bill 540 (AB 540) and the Dream Act. George Washington Carver Middle School, the Center Theater Group, and ArtsBridge collaborated to present the play, welcomed the students to campus with a university tour, and held a roundtable discussion with student leaders about AB 540. Students, teachers, and administrators learned that undocumented students can indeed attend university in California and pay local tuition as a result of this legislation. However, because the Dream Act had not passed through the legislature, undocumented students still cannot receive public financial aid, nor get a driver's license, nor hold a job recognized through social security. In other words, currently undocumented students who can both finance and prepare themselves through university study cannot legally work in their field. However, with diligent personal and social action that, too, will change.

The positive impact of the collaboration was instantaneous and mutual. UCLA students were pleased to meet teenagers who were asking the hard questions regarding educational access for undocumented youth. The teenagers were inspired by the struggles and activism of undocumented university students who overcame tremendous odds to pursue their dreams. Classroom teachers, teaching artists, and school administrators who were unaware of the AB 540 legislation learned about options for undocumented students and can now better advise parents and future students. Finally, the performance and roundtable made it clear to participants how social change happens—through consistent dedicated effort over time. Undocumented students have the right to an education and it is a sign of civic responsibility to inform oneself and demand educational rights for all. Everyone present, children and adults alike, rededicated themselves to the struggle to increase educational opportunities for undocumented students through public action.

Another example of the connection between personal and social change can be felt during participatory evaluation. Our evaluation process included time together on the ground in each other's communities, as well as focus groups and preliminary and post surveys to set out aims and analyze our progress. During focus groups, teenage ArtsBridge students from South Los Angeles were invit-

Self-portrait taken by student during visit to college

ed into boardrooms at UCLA along with school district representatives, classroom teachers, UCLA Arts students, and staff. This participatory process reinforced the core values of intergenerational and intercultural connections. The evaluation process strengthened my view that having diverse participants at the table for decision-making enhances the perspectives available to the group and increases the likelihood that we understand and follow a more inclusive "truth."

One case in point involved a young dancer with a radiant smile and a shaved head who was particularly pleased to visit a university for the first time. While school and district administrators described the value of Arts-Bridge community partnerships in terms of standards achieved, he offered feedback that focused the group on its higher purpose. "ArtsBridge helps students find their true self," he scrawled in blue ink on the whiteboard. His opinion became our guiding force for evaluation. In fact, we found that the most dramatic quantifiable impact the program had was on increasing participants' positive views of themselves and their peers.[6]

Is feeling good about oneself and one's community politically valuable? For individuals and groups who are consistently misrepresented, left out, or silenced from larger public debate the answer is most definitely affirmative. Learning to value ourselves and others is a crucial precursor to create mutually beneficial partnerships be-

tween an expanded circle of community and university partners.

Curriculum for the whole human being

Together, we addressed cultural reclamation and re-invention by creating culturally and socially relevant learning opportunities for youth that are often misrepresented in, or excluded from, dominant educational and artistic paradigms. Participants both affirmed and stretched their own knowledge through culturally relevant curriculum. Cynthia Wennstrom, a visual artist of Filipino and Anglo descent, made sense of the cross-cultural dimensions of her ArtsBridge experience through poetry:

> I come from a people who grow bananas and potatoes.
>
> I study in a university where people frolic in country club beauty.
>
> I teach young people who want to dance in their own skins.
>
> I work with teachers who care about picking up the phone.
>
> I bring to ArtsBridge an open cup.
>
> I bring to my classroom pieces of a puzzle.[7]

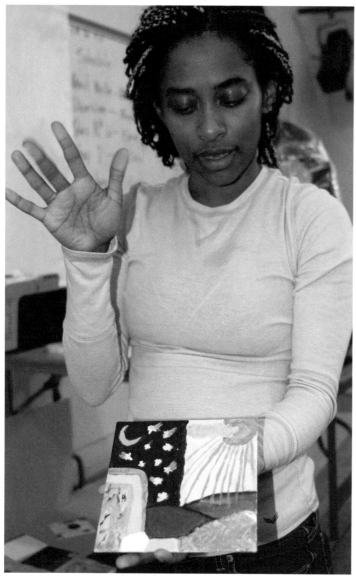

Tameka Norris reflects on her students' work

ArtsBridge partner teacher Kori Hamilton worked with ArtsBridge Scholars Iliana Phirippidis and Jena McRae to teach drama and language arts. They found that students better understood class reading when they analyzed it through dramatic play. For example, students read Laura Esquivel's novel *Like Water for Chocolate* (*Como Agua Para Chocolate*) and researched popular recipes from their own families. They then dramatized these recipes in skits and short videos such as "The Taco King" and "Daddy's Famous French Fries." This enriched the students' understanding of academic literature by relating it to their own lives, and helped them rehearse the important leadership skills of group cooperation and public speaking.

Healing also took place when students were encouraged to include personal reflections in their artistic productions. For example, ArtsBridge Scholar Tameka Norris developed a residency titled Finding Meaning in College-Bound Words through Visual Art. Students ferreted out words that high school students are tested on for college entrance examinations, but rarely hear in everyday English. As the students studied new words, and represented their meaning in paintings, the images they painted evoked real-life stories from each young person's life. Norris explained how her art classes at Jordan High School regularly evoked cathartic stories and tears among her students. "I feel that the most powerful and authentic works came from . . . allowing a story to emerge from the medium," wrote Norris.[8] Safe spaces for reflection and healing grew inside the arts classroom.

While high school dropout rates in LAUSD are about 26 percent overall (2007–2008), over half of the student body at our partner schools dropped out before graduating.[9] The art project allowed students to reveal the issues that impacted their lives and ability to succeed in school. One student in particular who had difficulty attending class consistently covered the background of her painting in black. Norris interpreted this student's work in the following way:

> . . . two red hearts floated at the upper and lower corners of the canvas. The upper heart was free and full, while the other lower heart was confined behind bars with a lock with no key. [The student] offered in critique that her boyfriend is in jail and probably will be for many years to come. She at-

In addition to cultural differences, cultural commonalities also fortify relationships between ArtsBridge Scholars and community partners. ArtsBridge Scholar Alicia Paniagua taught a Salsa in the Americas curriculum with Millikan Middle School students who are enrolled in English Language Learning (ELL) classes. Her aim was to inspire young bilingual students through her own example. Paniagua energized her teaching with her three passions: salsa dancing, Spanish language, and Latin American studies. Salsa instruction provided an important creative outlet for ELL students who were regularly denied access to an arts elective, and promoted their culture and skills within the larger school community.

tends court hearings, knows all the court jargon and does what she can to help him stay in good spirits. Additionally she has seven siblings that she has to get ready for school daily[10]

These examples demonstrate how creativity is a healing tool that helps connect students' real lives to the school curriculum. Creativity offers social and personal benefits that are central to enjoying and finding deeper meaning in education. By the end of the four-year collaboration with Hamilton's classroom, at least four of her students were college bound, and one headed straight to UCLA as a freshman.

Historically, "informal" learning normally takes place in the home or neighborhood, while "formal" learning takes place in school. Informal learning often recognizes cultural knowledge that formal schooling may undervalue or even prohibit. Since knowledge is tied to power relations, affirming different epistemologies (ways of knowing) is an important outcome of creative cultural education.

We committed ourselves to bridging informal and formal learning by validating culturally grounded knowledge gained outside of school while also fulfilling formal requirements for study. One example of this took place when a middle school student at Millikan Middle School made vivid connections between her life at school and in her community through a visual arts exercise in collage with ArtsBridge Scholar Cynthia Wennstrom. The strips of color she used reminded her of the wings of a bird, and nearly flew right off of the page. Jasmine's artwork was inspired by a freedom song she sang in church on weekends. After telling the story of how she felt while singing that song in church, she sang the same song out loud to her teacher and classmates. In that moment, a young woman who struggled with reading and writing at grade level reclaimed her dignity by demonstrating she was a powerful communicator through song and image. Her role in the classroom shifted when she could finally be seen for her strengths. On the whole, after six months of visual arts study, this Directed Reading and Writing classroom improved its language skills on comprehensive tests from grade three to grade six levels. The classroom teacher, and the school vice principal, Leah Bass-Bayliss, attributed this improvement directly to studying art because no other change had been made to their instructional plan.

Another example of how art-making inspired spiritual empowerment took place in a sculpture class facilitated by ArtsBridge Scholar Karen Huang and classroom teacher Alix Fournier at John Muir Middle School. Students wrote stories about imaginary creatures with special powers and then brought them to life in clay. Many of the pieces had deep spiritual significance to the youth. Ramona, an eighth grader, made a sculpture she called the *Moses of Love*. She explained, it is "a symbol of luck because it likes to help people with their problems." Her creation that "only helps people who are nice and not mean," included a spherical form containing a sequined heart with an eye in its center, rabbit ears, wings, and a snake-like tail. Through her sculpture, Ramona invented an art piece that focused her desire for power over her daily life.

Akeba Jackson, a partner teacher at Dorsey High School, told the story of a high school student who complained when he was removed from her drama class that was supplanted with a computer course. He told the counselor, "I need drama." "No you don't. You need computers," the counselor rebuked. "No, I *need* drama," he emphasized. The young man explained to me that they talk about emotions in Ms. Jackson's drama class. He also added, "My teacher does not have to care about me when school gets out at 3:05, but she does. She is not even my family, but she cares, and that makes me want to work that much harder." His response raises a crucial point. A quality education should be a sensate experience that cultivates the whole person including one's values, mind, body, and emotions.

Movement literacy

Different artistic mediums require specific "literacies" that are comparable in importance to the more recognized areas of writing, reading, or computation. Movement education challenges deeply seated stereotypes about knowledge, the body, and identity. The legacy of Cartesian thinking still undergirds many scholastic programs that fail to acknowledge that learning involves complex connections between the mind, body, and the emotions. Not surprisingly, it is common to encounter difficulties gaining support for dance education among school administrators and teachers. Dance education fosters corporeal learning that requires putting one's own body on the line for learn-

Desireé Gallardo teaches Polynesian dance to students at Santa Monica High School

ing. One's body becomes the artistic medium itself—the palette and the page.

The process of dance choreography and presentation can become a forum for social analysis, public commentary, and public debate. A dance theater piece choreographed by Jordan High School students, under the guidance of classroom teacher Monzell Corley, was set to the music of Michael Jackson's well-known music video *Thriller*. However, the students structured their own version of *Thriller* set in a local public hospital. Martin Luther King / Drew Medical Center Hospital, often nicknamed "Killer King" by residents, was sited for serious deficiencies in care that threatened patients' lives. Ironically, the struggling hospital was built with the hopes of serving the community and named after the noted civil rights leader Dr. Martin Luther King Jr. and Dr. Charles Richard Drew, a path-breaking African American medical scientist. Current events that are normally relegated to newspaper columns became a hot topic at school as a result of the students' public performance. Youth presented their original work on Halloween for the larger school community to the infectious sounds of a classic music video. Dancers

playing patients were heaped in piles on the floor as they wallowed in pain and then rose to dance to a compelling beat as mummies and ghouls. Movements included a doctor/dancer ripping a fake baby from another performer's belly and throwing it across the stage irreverently. Both the creative and performative processes that invigorated the dance composition fostered critical thinking about the quality of social services in South Los Angeles through the language of dance. Student enthusiasm for learning was demonstrated through their work on a significant public health issue.

In the United States, legislation exists that stipulates equitable access to physical education for both boys and girls. An outcome of the women's movement, Title IX was passed in 1972 and requires gender equity for boys and girls including access to higher education, athletics, career education, education for pregnant and parenting students, among other areas. The core legislation states,

No person in the United States shall, on the basis of sex, be excluded from participation in, be denied the benefits of, or be subjected to discrimi-

Raúl Ortega performs at South Los Angeles Dance Conference

nation under any education program or activity receiving federal financial assistance.[11]

Access to dance education in Los Angeles is limited as it has fallen into a chasm between fine arts and physical education mandates—a problem that is further exacerbated by the lack of a Californian dance teaching credential. In addition, gender stereotypes continue to limit access to movement expression for girls and boys. One vivid example took place in a high school where ArtsBridge helped a school district implement their first dance education endowment. The district chose to focus on secondary dance training through physical education. The initial response from the school was that dance could only be taught to girls because boys would reject the opportunity. Ninth-grade girls would be offered dance while ninth-grade boys would study weight training. The school quietly permitted unequal standards of participation when ninth-grade boys weren't allowed to dance, and girls weren't encouraged to lift weights during their first year of high school. ArtsBridge took the position that we would only collaborate with the school district if dance education were offered to both boys and girls.

This experience allowed us to challenge outdated gender roles about who wants to dance. While our position on dance as a coeducational activity was initially seen as confrontational, the school quickly warmed up to the idea of boys dancing when they saw the program in action. By the end of the dance residency, the physical education (PE) director, who was also the school's football coach, became convinced that dance could be offered for both boys and girls. In a communal electronic journal he wrote:

> [We] were enthralled with today's dance. I think many of the students, particularly boys, felt much more relevance to this [hip hop] movement because it's something they see everyday. Today showed me what I believed, but needed to see. Dance on any campus can be big.[12]

Dance is also a valuable forum for teaching cultural studies. ArtsBridge Scholar Desiree Gallardo taught Hawaiian and Polynesian dance forms to help students gain a new respect for Pacific Island culture and values while making connections with their own family backgrounds. Gallardo explains,

Not only did they learn how to do the steps, but they learned how to spell the names of each step that I taught them—*kaholo*, *kalakaua*, *hela*, and *uehe*. . . . These exercises make connections of sound through spelling the Hawaiian language and listening to two different hula music/dance styles.[13]

These examples demonstrate how schools benefited from including dance education as an academic subject. Whether embodying social commentary, crossing gender roles, or learning cultural history through movement, dance education expanded the participants' understanding of the connections between movement, culture, and history.

Media studies

Media literacy is a crucial skill for youth who are bombarded with media messages but do not always learn how to critique them or create their own. Understanding media and technology can be supported by knowledge of design and visual art concepts. An ArtsBridge residency at David Starr Jordan High School connected geometry teacher Bill Branscomb to ArtsBridge Scholars Audrey Ma and Erin Jacobs who introduced his tenth-grade students to basic spatial design concepts and computer skills. Students created collages of their lives that used text and imagery to create media messages about what they valued. Students chose to focus on recent mass mobilizations for immigrant rights, the importance of steadfast friends, the tragedy of Hurricane Katrina, the importance of staying connected to one's cultural roots, and anxieties about transitioning from childhood into adulthood. Mr. Branscomb was impressed by the creativity that flowed from his students. He compared the process of studying design to ripening student learning from mere grapes into a rich wine.

This introductory design experience was linked to college preparation when three design students were invited to continue their studies at the UCLA Summer Design Institute. Scholarships were provided by UCLA's Summer Programs Office, and high school students were able to study music video and game design in college. Rogelio Acevedo, education coordinator at the Watts Towers Arts Center near the high school, hosted a college arts orientation for students and families before they headed out to UCLA to study.

Despite the positive overall experience, obstacles did need to be overcome. Initially, no female high school students applied for the scholarship since girls were not provided the same liberties by their parents as their male counterparts. Special attention was required to facilitate participation among girls by close conversations with their guardians. Also, bringing students together at UCLA did not blur the existence of privilege and inequality. In her exit interview, high school student Sonia Balonas commented that the other students were familiar with the advanced programs while she had never seen them before. She was slowed down by having to aimlessly press random buttons on the computer screen to decipher the functions while her peers seemed to navigate through the program with greater ease. Thankfully, the following year a nonprofit organization, the Media Aid Center under the direction of Martin Cheeseborough, brought a fully functional media lab to their school. Now many students are gaining the preparation they deserve year round. Efforts like these will begin to close the digital divide that exists between schools and communities.

Despite the challenges, students showed tenacity, created original work, experienced college life, and earned college credit that would reflect well on future university applications. "I always wanted to learn how to make video games," explained David Scoggins, "and I got tired of people telling me I couldn't do something." After making her own music video, Balonas reflected,

I learned that I never knew I could get so nervous under pressure and around strangers. I never knew I could be so shy. I learned that it doesn't really matter . . . if you have not done it before. If you apply yourself, you really try, and once in a while ask for help, you can get anything done.[14]

Balonas's parents were very supportive and pleased with her studies at UCLA. "We need more programs like this to give opportunities," Mr. Balonas said. They invited me to celebrate her coming of age in a *quinceañera* celebration later that summer, which was an impressive event. Editing and directing a music video, experiencing college life, and celebrating her transition into young adulthood, all contributed to her important rites of passage.[15]

As of 2010, LAUSD documented ninety-three different languages spoken by their student body. However, the overwhelming majority of bilingual LAUSD students are Spanish speakers. A champion for bilingual education, Kris Gutierrez raises the important point that every student who studies English, whether it is their first language or not, is an English-language learner.[16] The official terminology used to designate bilingual students reflects the heated discourse about bilingual education in a state that all too often depicts bilingual or polyglot students from a deficiency perspective rather than an asset-based perspective. The bilingual education movement, in many ways inspired by the Chicano and immigrant rights movements, continues to advocate for the value of bilingualism as a useful skill set rather than a problem.

In California public schools, students who are not reading and writing at grade level, were introduced to English later in life, or live in households where English is not the dominant tongue are often placed in ELL classes and required to study English twice a day at the expense of other subject areas such as science or the arts. As a result, many ELL students are systematically denied the opportunity to study dance, music, drama, or art. Ironically, in the effort to increase English language instructional hours students are denied creative outlets for literacy development through the arts.

ArtsBridge Scholars Brittany Maxwell and Laurel Bybee constructed design curriculum for middle school students in eighth-grade history, and for students that have been assigned to what is called an ELL class. Working with a middle school ELL class, Bybee developed three activities that introduced students to the new environment of Adobe Illustrator. First, she instructed students in typography by learning about font families and constructing a font family tree affirming their design skills along with their own genealogy and geographical origin. The second assignment introduced students to the camera and created original self-portraits. Finally, their typography skills and portraits were used to create bilingual posters in English and their language of origin. The creative student work highlighted their bilingualism in a positive light. The bilingual posters helped ELL students represent themselves to the larger school community on their own terms visual-ly and linguistically. Clearly, media studies provides valuable opportunities for language development along with computer literacy, and offers new platforms for expressing personal and public opinions.

Connecting the dots

Oscar Neal, a Jordan High School alumnus and Watts community leader, described community-building through the arts as "connecting the dots." For Neal, crossing over the borders within our city's educational system would change the map of Los Angeles, converting our communities from tiny "dots" on an urban grid to living relationships between real people and places. He explained to a gathering of ArtsBridge partners from across the city,

> If I look around the circle here we are beginning to connect the dots. . . . It is very important to understand that we all have an obligation and a duty to give back . . . and in doing that we fulfill some of the things of our life ambition.[17]

International connections pulse through the bloodlines, and immigrant stories of Los Angeles' residents. At the Chiapas gathering, I was touched by the story of a young man at UniTierra (University of the Land) whose father had left the family to find alternative employment in the United States. The pain that coated his voice from his father's absence was palpable. He explained that he had temporarily lost his ability to speak and move his arm. Slowly, while studying at UniTierra, he overcame his silence, and was now able to share his story with us. Even though I had traveled by plane, car, and foot to visit his community, his father might be living or working next door to me in Los Angeles. The earth and water are borderless, and many of our families are too. Resilient family ties are sustained despite migration and immigration. People are not simple "dots" on a map, but living connections within our regional ecosystem. I could never begin to understand the city of Los Angeles without understanding how its threads are woven into the very fabric of our broader regional landscape.

CHAPTER 8

WITH OUR IMAGES, VOICES, AND CULTURES

BilwiVision—A Community Television Channel

Margarita Antonio and Reyna Armida Duarte
URACCAN, Bilwi, Nicaragua

A little history

Many forces have shaped the multiethnic, multilingual, and multicultural society found today on the Nicaraguan Caribbean Coast—the stubborn perseverance of the peoples who inhabited the area during the colonial period, the initial relationships of cooperation with the explorers and later with the British Crown, as well as the migration of new peoples to the region.

The emergence of the Nicaraguan nation and the annexation of the Caribbean Coast by military intervention brought about a new period in Nicaraguan history. Ever since, women and men in the region have demanded respect for their historic rights. The civil war at the end of the twentieth century during the Sandinista Revolution ultimately led to granting of legal autonomy to the Coast.

Through the election and establishment of regional councils and governments, autonomous rights were strengthened. This happened simultaneously with the emergence of new initiatives and institutions aimed at contributing to the development of the Caribbean Coast. In the area of education, the creation of URACCAN, the University of the Autonomous Regions of the Nicaraguan Caribbean Coast, is a special example.

URACCAN initiated processes in which teaching, research, and community outreach were combined in order to better promote regional development. This synergy contributed to the strengthening of autonomous rights through the development of peoples' potential and abilities.

With the support of the Canadian government, York University, based in Toronto, was one of the first postsecondary institutions in North America to establish a partnership with URACCAN, offering graduate education to faculty members. This alliance contributed to the development of peoples' capabilities as they undertook research within intercultural and multidisciplinary contexts.

A unique communications program

Within the field of communications, URACCAN promoted a variety of initiatives. It established community radio stations in areas where previously they did not exist and trained journalists within the communities on the use and management of these stations, respecting their own culture, identity, language, and cosmovision. It also promoted access to new information technology and communication opportunities so the national media, based in the capital city of Managua, would cover the historical process of autonomy. As a part of this effort, the university started a Bilwi-based audiovisual production program in 2000 with the support of a city-to-city partnership between Burlington, Vermont, and Bilwi (also known as Puerto Cabezas).

Bilwi is the capital of the autonomous North Atlantic Region. Its almost fifty thousand residents belong to the Miskitu, Creole, Sumu-mayangna, and Mestizo ethnic

Fisherman on the Caribbean coast of Nicaragua

groups, each one of them preserving their own language and culture. Before 2006, there was no national television reception in Bilwi.

This, however, was not problematic since mainstream channels rarely reflect the cultural reality of the Caribbean Coast. A similar process is repeated in most urban settings on the Coast, where there is a broad range of cable TV channels that do not offer programs of interest to local communities.

As a part of the audiovisual production in Bilwi, the local cable company began transmitting a university-based TV program. In the beginning of 2005, the cable company proposed that the university operate a local TV channel in partnership with them. URACCAN accepted

Miskitu grandmother with her grandchildren, Tuapi

the proposal, and community members were trained to produce programs that would promote intercultural relationships, with the participation of people of diverse ethnic backgrounds, cultures, languages, genders, and ages.

When URACCAN was ready to launch the new TV channel, however, the cable company decided instead to rent the TV channel to the university. While most cable companies fund local TV productions, this was not the

case in Bilwi, with URACCAN ultimately having to cover all the operational costs.

BilwiVision is born

URACCAN continued to develop BilwiVision, which was finally launched in June 2005. We have been serving the Bilwi community since then and can identify both achievements and challenges inherent to the project, as well as lessons we have learned.

Before starting the official transmissions, we worked for three months to figure out what we wanted from a com-

above left: URACCAN University near Bilwi, Nicaragua

below left: Homes in Miskitu village of Krukira in northeastern Nicaragua

BilwiVision team, with Duarte second from right.

munity TV channel. What should it be? We did surveys seeking the opinions of young people, women, men, children, government employees, scholars, and even some politicians. We learned how to operate TV cameras, we overcame stage fright and ultimately we decided that our channel would include all the languages spoken in the region.

With these ideas in mind, we developed a daily schedule that would serve as a foundation for a pilot program, a model for subsequent programs to be gradually added to as we grew. We included news, comments, interviews, sports, health, and variety shows. From the start, we also produced programs in the Miskitu and Creole languages as well as Spanish.

The idea was that, eventually, each of these segments could evolve to become a program on its own. Right from the beginning, women organized and produced their own program. Likewise, some local journalists produced their own news shows.

Each one of the programs produced at BilwiVision represents a special effort of collective creation. Fortunately, we do not count on "experts" to produce any of our programs; we are learning together and we are aware of what we do not want to do. For this reason, the most important quality of the team members is their personal commitment and their willingness to participate.

Reyna Armida Duarte filming an interview with a fisherman in Krukira

EPILOGUE

CRITICAL HOPE

Deborah Barndt

Five years have passed since VIVA! partners gathered at the Indigenous UniTierra (University of the Land) in Chiapas, Mexico, for our third and final funded gathering in 2006, where we first shared and discussed our videos and draft chapters for this book. Nothing stands still, and all of the projects described here have evolved; while some have faded or dissolved, most have morphed into new and expanding programs.

Two moments in the spring of 2010 best exemplify the burgeoning of community arts as a field and a practice integral to research and education, and illustrate the ongoing creative tensions we confront in this work aimed at social transformation. One story comes from the Global North, from the home base of the VIVA! project, York University, and its Community Arts Practice program. The other comes from the Global South, where VIVA! partner URACCAN recently hosted the fourth international encounter of the project on the Caribbean Coast of Nicaragua. Both embody, but in quite different ways, the deepening contradiction of increasingly neoliberal market-driven universities that at the same time promote community engagement and knowledge production for autonomy and social justice. Both offer what Panamanian collaborator Raúl Leis calls "critical hope,"[1] integrating a recognition of the structural constraints with a creative capacity to find the possibilities within them.

Moment 1: York University, Canada

Since 2005 and parallel to the VIVA! project, we have been crafting a program in community arts practice (CAP) at York University.[2] Central to the initiative is an interdisciplinary certificate, jointly administered by the Faculty of Environmental Studies and the Faculty of Fine Arts. The first of its kind in Canada, the CAP certificate is open not only to all undergraduate students at York, but also to people with an undergraduate degree or equivalent experience in the community arts field, who can complete the twenty-four–credit certificate part-time over two years. Three core courses, starting with Community Arts for Social Change and culminating in a fourth-year practicum or internship with a community arts project, are supplemented with electives from four categories: community and popular education, critical social analysis, an introductory studio course in an artistic discipline, and an advanced community arts studio course.

Much beyond the certificate itself and undergrad classes, the broader CAP program integrates four interrelated components: collaborative research, teaching (including graduate courses), public education, and networking for arts advocacy. Community partners—both artists and social justice organizations—have helped shape the program from the start, are key advisors and hosts for student placements, and often collaborate on public seminars or workshops. In January 2010, for exam-

"Letters from the Dead" street performance, Toronto, 2007

storytelling workshops with immigrant women, done arts administration with a major community arts organization, and animated art-making workshops within a social housing project. The energy, connection, and engagement generated by the collaborations have been striking. In the coming year, CAP students will be interning with a black theater company, a documentary film production company, a community photography gallery, an activist group advocating for undocumented workers, an arts program within a neighborhood community center, and a puppet-based community theater program. The interdisciplinary program has created a space for cross-faculty as well as community-university dialogue, for critical reflection and action. As a fine arts CAP student suggests:

> The CAP program offers learning beyond the classroom, and it extends the fine arts outside of the traditional institutions. Each student is an active facilitator and the public becomes engaged participants. A CAP class forces students to think critically and creatively, to really engage with contemporary societal and political issues, and to find innovative solutions.

An environmental studies graduate notes the two-way process the program generates:

> Not only does CAP empower students, it also draws traditionally marginalized communities into the university, creating new spaces for collaboration and dialogue.

As word of the program has spread, students from other faculties and practitioners from community arts organizations have entered. Yet, while the program is gaining momentum both within and outside of the university, it is not without both internal and external contradictions. CAP still draws primarily white middle-class students, and mostly young women. Our efforts to recruit students from marginalized or racialized communities, for example, are often thwarted by the pressures second-generation Canadians face first to be admitted into and pay tuition to postsecondary education institutions and then to seek more "practical" and lucrative careers, to live out their parents' dreams that their

ple, we organized a conference with community partners in Toronto, Shooting Back: Photography, Participation, and Power: Celebrating and Challenging Photo Voice and Digital Storytelling, and hosted film screenings on themes ranging from spirituality and activism to the history of legal struggles by the LGBT community. In the 2010–2011 academic year, CAP students contributed artistic skills to a major campaign for food literacy and facilitated arts-based workshops for a forum on gender-based violence with 150 high school students from the neighborhood where York University is located.

What does a CAP placement look like? Over the past year, students have developed theater programs with developmentally disabled youth, facilitated digital lives will be more successful in social status and financial terms. Within our classes, students are often motivated by a charity notion of social change, and while honoring the impulse, we are challenged to help them develop a more critical social analysis of the historical and structural causes of the power relations we work to transform. At the same time, we promote self-reflexivity among students to reflect on their own identities and power relations within the groups they work with.

Equity issues arise not only in the recruitment of students, but also in the hiring of instructors; although there is an affirmative action policy, activists/artists/academics of color are limited in number, again due to structural discrimination, as well as institutionalized racism. Members of hiring committees, for example, tend to reproduce themselves, not always open to the diverse ways of knowing and cultural expression that might broaden our program's response to Toronto's diasporic population.

Externally, York University faculty and students are witnessing several troubling trends:

- The deepening corporatization of the neoliberal-driven university, with eroding public funding and increasingly more dependence on private monies and interests;

- The prioritizing of federal and provincial monies for science and technology, business and law, with diminishing support for the humanities, arts, and social sciences;

- The measurement of successful teaching reduced to the number of "bums in seats" and of successful research reduced to the amount of state-supported academic research monies secured;

- An increasingly market-driven curriculum that assumes that graduates' obtaining a well-paying job is the ultimate mission of universities in the twenty-first century.

York University was founded over fifty years ago with a commitment to social justice. It proudly touts the most diverse student body in the country, and promotes itself as the interdisciplinary university. A recent white paper, developed through consultation with the York community, proposes the new moniker of "the engaged university," highlighting community-university collaboration and experiential learning.[3] Yet we were advised in the spring of 2010 that if a program can't pay for itself, in terms of "bums in seats" and/or external research monies, it can be eliminated. Our Community Arts Practice program, which epitomizes the mantra of experiential community-engaged learning based on community-university collaboration, is threatened because it isn't sufficiently income producing.

We are not alone in facing this contradiction. The threat became very real for one of our academic partners in the VIVA! project: UCLA eliminated the coordinator's position of the ArtsBridge program in 2009, due to cutbacks. Training arts educators to work in inner-city schools just wasn't among the priorities of state funding bodies. NGOs are facing similar chilling responses; KAIROS, a national interchurch coalition in Canada, had half its funding cut by the Conservative government, clearly due to advocacy work that challenged government policies around climate change. Jumblies Theatre, a Toronto-based VIVA! collaborator, has been denied funding for community arts training, and other similar groups across Canada have noted the shifting priorities favoring elitist art and cultural institutions.

Philosopher Martha Nussbaum warns that the "growing obsession with knowledge that you can take to the bank" that eschews the teaching of critical thinking for quick fix technical training is coming back to haunt us; it has in fact led to the Wall Street economic collapse and the BP oil spill in the Gulf of Mexico. The humanities, arts, and social sciences are essential, Nussbaum contends, so students aren't "just accepting what's passed down from some kind of authority, but thinking critically about it, examining yourself and figuring out what you really want to stand for."[4] They bring richer meaning to life, nurture an empathetic understanding of differences among people, nurture active citizens, and, especially through the arts, train the imagination.

We have recently formed a new Arts and Communities network at York of activist/scholars from across the university who share a common concern about this erosion of the social purpose and public responsibility of universities. We will join forces in our defense of the space for critical thinking and creative collaboration between academics, artists, and activists. With our community partners, we are seeking ways to advocate for

VIVA! partners in Bilwi, Nicaragua, in April 2010:
Deborah Barndt, Margarita Antonio, Nancy Zuniga, Reyna Armida Duarte, José Angel Colman, Amy Shimshon-Santo.

more support for both formal and informal training in the arts for social justice. If these new alliances offer some grounds for "critical hope," our partners in the South face similar pressures, but with fewer resources and, in some cases, with greater resistance and imagination. Though the transnational research project is no longer funded, for example, it is clear that, in Nicaragua, VIVA! *vive* (lives) . . . !

Moment 2: URACCAN University, Nicaragua

At our third international exchange in Chiapas in late 2006, Margarita Antonio and Reyna Armida Duarte of URACCAN in Nicaragua offered to host the Fourth Encuentro (Encounter) of VIVA! on the Caribbean Coast of Nicaragua. However, Hurricane Felix hit the coast the following year, devastating the university, the BilwiVision

Miskitu youth leads urale, a ritual song and circle dance at the closing of the Encuentro, 2010

TV station, and many Indigenous communities. Nonetheless, by April of 2010, our Nicaraguan partners were ready to fulfill their promise. They were able to secure support from the Ford Foundation for the conference and for travel subsidies. Five of us VIVA! project partners made the trip to the coast—representing projects in Panama, Mexico, the United States, and Canada. We gathered along with one hundred others—poets and artists, students and professors from all over the country.

URACCAN was established in the 1990s as a community-based university, with a mission to promote self-determination and the pluriethnicity of the Miskitu, Creole, and mestizo populations in the newly autonomous regions of the coast. Forty of its faculty participated in the Encuentro, along with fifty high school students participating in a youth leadership training program mounted by the university. The Encuentro was very much in the spirit of the autonomy law, promoting intergenerational dialogue with local and national leaders about resisting cultural homogenization and recovering the histories, cultural values, and forms of artistic expression of their peoples (what they call "cultural revitalization"). Panel presentations allowed artists and educators from other parts of the country to share their work with community museums, mural projects, and cultural research resulting in sculpture parks depicting Indigenous ancestors and icons. Film screenings revealed the use of video to both celebrate and protest, from recreating Indigenous legends in native languages to exposing the racism and horrific conditions within a local prison. Public readings in the evening confirmed Nicaragua's reputation as a "country of poets." In other moments, Creole youth filled the room with the energy of their drums and dances; in an exhilarating closing ritual, Miskitu youth invited us all to join a call-and-response *urale* ritual song and circle dance.

The international component of the Encuentro focused on recent work by VIVA! partners, updating the information provided in the chapters of this book. In a keynote, I was able to share and briefly review the eight projects and introduce our Community Arts Practice program, as a possible model for university engagement in this field. Representing the Painting by Listening project in Mexico, Nancy Zuniga reported on the recent proliferation of workshops led by artist Checo Valdez training Indigenous people in Chiapas State in community mural production. Amy Shimshon-Santo demonstrated her commitment to this work through her response to the 2009 cutbacks in UCLA's ArtsBridge program; even though her coordinator position was eliminated, she worked voluntarily with student artists to self-publish a collection of stories based on their experiences teaching art in inner-city schools. In a unique transnational artistic dialogue, Panamanian Kuna partner José Colman has been collaborating with Monique Mojica, Toronto-based Kuna/Rappahanock actor and playwright, to create a theater based on Kuna cosmovision, images, legends, and creative processes; they shared their multilingual work-in-progress.

A highlight was the launch of the Spanish edition of the VIVA! book (an earlier version of this one). The production process was speeded up, and it impressed us that in a context with fewer resources, our Nicaraguan partners were able to get the Spanish book out before the English one! Another special experience was a visit to a nearby Miskitu village, Tuapi, talking with local leaders about their cultural development.

Finally, we spent two afternoons at the URACCAN campus with over forty faculty members (a majority) who shared their own artistic passions, and developed a plan of action for integrating arts and culture into the curriculum, research, and community work. The recommendations that came out of that action planning session are synthe-sized on page 130 under three categories: general thrusts, specific actions within URACCAN, and specific actions that the university could support in local schools.

It is striking how certain threads in these recommendations reinforce the key themes that emerged from the VIVA! project exchange: a broad concept of culture; the decolonization of a Eurocentric curriculum; the reclamation of local history, culture, and ways of knowing; the development of activities from, with, and for the community; interdisciplinary and inter-institutional collaboration.

It's hard to imagine a similar undertaking at a university in the Global North—getting local and national officials, artists, and university faculty members to exchange experiences and ideas about how to promote community arts within the university and surrounding communities. Yet in Nicaragua they came together for three days to do precisely that—to examine how their curriculum could recover histories, revalue cultures, catalyze critical thinking about social issues, and inspire people to create many forms of expression that strengthen cultural identity and community development. They took the deeper purposes of the VIVA! project seriously and gave them new meaning even in a context of scarcity and exclusion.

This creative process was not stifled by the multiple pressures that neoliberalism has put on universities (in the South just as in the North), nor was it dismissed as futile because there are so few resources available in this marginalized region. There is a strong sense of "critical hope" here that acknowledges the political, economic, and social contradictions and tensions, but that ultimately understands that the greatest resources are human, and take the form of commitment, creativity, and imagination. This is perhaps one of the greatest values of our intercultural exchange with Latin American popular educators and community artists: to deepen our own critical analysis while nurturing our own sense of hope.

URACCAN Action Plan Proposal

General thrusts

1. Promote a very broad concept of "culture," which is pluriethnic, inclusive, local, and dynamic, and includes not only visual arts, music, dance, theater, and literature, but also spiritual and emotional expressions, ways of life, values and beliefs (for example, culinary arts, cultural knowledge such as traditional medicine, among others);

2. Create our own integrated cultural program for the autonomous regions, integrating art and culture into all development programs;

3. Consider artistic and cultural development as development goals in themselves, indispensable to a full life, not merely decoration, entertainment, or a means to an end;

4. In public spaces, facilitate artistic experiences that are drawn from the community and engage community members;

5. Strengthen our capacity to recover and reclaim cultural practices, drawing on the wisdom of our elders in this process;

6. Integrate art with environmental themes;

7. Promote inter-institutional collaboration between universities and cultural centers to share experiences and technical skills;

8. Reestablish cultural centers (Casas de Cultura) throughout the region;

9. Consider art and culture as inherent rights and defend intellectual property rights to guard against commercial abuse and other kinds of appropriation.

Actions within URACCAN

1. Organize workshops in dance, music, visual arts, and so forth, with and for the community;

2. Develop the artistic cultural field as a career and department with well-trained instructors;

3. Integrate art into the curriculum of all other fields of study;

4. Decolonize our teaching of history, focusing less on the official national history and more on the history of the region and local communities;

5. Challenge the classical colonial categories and transform academic spaces and rituals—for example, including emotional and spiritual development, integrating research and teaching, theory and practice;

6. Promote links between the university and community through internships;

7. Involve communities actively in all of the new cultural initiatives;

8. Use information technology and new media to support these processes;

9. Better promote our existing cultural programs, like the leadership school, and include our alumni in diverse cultural activities.

Specific actions in public schools

1. Support primary and secondary school teachers to integrate artistic activities with local content in all their curriculum (a recent curriculum reform allows 30 percent local content to be developed by the teacher);

2. Integrate the arts into the history curriculum, broadening it conceptually to include oral history, community history, daily social and cultural history;

3. Build on the Ministry of Education's plan to organize workshops in the communities in song, poetry, and handicraft production.

Notes

Preface: Who, Why and How VIVA?

1. Thomas King, The Truth About Stories (Toronto: Anansi Press, 2003), 32.

2. In his Nobel Peace Prize speech, Chilean poet Pablo Neruda declared: "Our original guiding stars are struggle and hope." http://cs80.wordpress.com/about/pablo-neruda-nobel-prize-speech/, accessed June 30, 2010.

3. Some would call the VIVA! Project "translocal" rather than transnational, as it links local projects across borders.

4. In the lead-up to the Mexican federal election of 2006, Mexican police attacked two communities near Mexico City, Texcoco and Atenco, both resisting corporate development on community land. Police violence resulted in the deaths of two young people and in the sexual assault of female detainees. These actions were widely condemned by Mexican and international human rights organizations.

5. The caracol or conch shell is also an instrument of communication among Indigenous communities, used to call people together. It is also appropriate that caracol is the word Zapatistas use for the communities they've formed in autonomous or free zones. The symbol thus represents both community and community art or cultural tools of expression.

Introduction: Rooted in Place, Politics, Passion, and Praxis

1. I am grateful to Monique Mojica, Rappahannock-Kuna actor and playwright, for pointing out that my original framework of three components reproduced the trinity or triangle of Judeo-Christian thought with an implicit hierarchy, and for suggesting that four components might better represent the balance contained within a circle, or spiral. This circle echoes Medicine Wheel teachings of several First Nations peoples; I have drawn in particular from the Ojibwe teachings; see http://www.fourdirectionsteachings.com/main.html, accessed June 15, 2010.

2. All of the quotes by VIVA! partners in this chapter are from transcripts of our third annual gathering held at Universidad de la Tierra in San Cristóbal de las Casas, Chiapas, Mexico in December 2006.

3. These structural inequities did not begin in 1492; scholars of precolonial history have confirmed the hierarchical dynamics, such as patriarchy, in many other civilizations; see Charles Mann, 1491: New Revelations of the Native Americans Before Columbus (New York: Knopf, 2005); Ronald Wright, A Short History of Progress (Toronto: House of Anansi Press, 2004).

4. Ania Loomba, Colonialism/Postcolonialism (New York: Routledge, 2005), 91.

5. Laura Reinsborough and Deborah Barndt, "Decolonizing Art, Education and Research in the VIVA! Project," Re/Envisioning Relationships, ed. L. Davis (Toronto: University of Toronto Press), 158–177.

6. Linda Tuhiwai Smith, Decolonizing Methodologies: Research and Indigenous Peoples (New York: Zed Books, 1999), 21.

7. Frantz Fanon, The Wretched of the Earth (New York: Grove Atlantic, 2005).

8. Loomba, Colonialism/Postcolonialism.

9. Robert Young, Postcolonialism: A Very Short Introduction (Oxford, UK: Oxford University Press, 2003).

10. Gayatri Spivak, "Can the Subaltern Speak?" Marxism and the Interpretation of Culture, ed. Cary Nelson and Lawrence Grossberg (Champaign: University of Illinois Press, 1988).

11. Diana Taylor, The Archive and the Repertoire: Performing Cultural Memory in the Americas (Durham, NC: Duke University Press, 2003), 34.

12. Ibid., 15.

13. Gregory Cajete, "Seeing the Voices of Our Heart: The Visionary and Artistic Foundations of Tribal Education," Look to the Mountain: An Ecology of Indigenous Education (Asheville, NC: Kivaki Press, 1994), 142–164.

14. Eleanor Heartney, "Native Identity in an Age of Hybridity," Remix: New Modernities in a Post-Indian World, ed. Joe Baker and Gerald McMaster (Washington, DC/New York: National Museum of the American Indian/Smithsonian Institution, 2007), 37–53.

15. Susan Strega, "The View from the Poststructural Margins: Epistemology and Methodology Reconsidered," Research as Resistance: Critical, Indigenous and Anti-Oppressive Approaches, ed. Leslie Brown and Susan Strega (Toronto: Canadian Scholars' Press, 2005), 203.

16. Parts of this chapter draw from Deborah Barndt, "Remapping the Americas: A Transnational Engagement with Creative Tensions of Community Arts," Critical Transnational Feminist Praxis, ed. R. Nagar and A. Swarr (Albany: State University of New York Press, 2010), 166–191.

17. Robin D. G. Kelley, Freedom Dreams: The Black Radical Imagination (Boston: Beacon Press, 2002), 196.

18. Myles Horton is recognized as the Paulo Freire of North America, and the Highlander Research and Education Center bears a seventy-seven-year legacy of radical educational practice. See www.highlandercenter.org.

19. Myles Horton, The Long Haul (New York: Teachers College Press, 1998), 131.

20. Valerie Miller, Between Struggle and Hope: The Nicaraguan Literacy Crusade (Boulder and London: Westview Press, 1985).

21. Deborah Barndt, To Change This House: Popular Education under the Sandinistas (Toronto: Between the Lines, 1991).

22. dian marino, Wild Garden: Art, Education and the Culture of Resistance (Toronto: Between the Lines, 1997), 20.

23. Patricia Hill Collins, Black Feminist Thought: Knowledge, Consciousness and the Politics of Empowerment (London/New York: Routledge, 1991).

24. Daniel Schugurensky, "The Legacy of Paulo Freire: A Critical Review of His Contributions," Convergence: International Journal of Adult Education 31.1, 2 (1998): 17–29.

25. bell hooks, Teaching to Transgress: Education as the Practice of Freedom (London: Routledge, 1994), 50.

26. Deborah Barndt, Education and Social Change: A Photographic Study of Peru (Dubuque: Kendal-Hunt Publishing, 1980).

27. Paulo Freire, Pedagogy of the Oppressed (New York: Continuum, 2007).

28. www.cepalforja.org.

29. Rick Arnold, Deborah Barndt, and Bev Burke, A New Weave: Popular Education in Canada and Central America (Ottawa: Canadian University Overseas; and Toronto: Ontario Institute for Studies in Education, 1985).

30. Graciela Bustos and Laura Vargas, Técnicas Participativas de Educación Popular (Guadalajara: IMDEC, 1988).

31. Bev Burke, Jojo Geronimo, D'Arcy Martin, Barb Thomas, and Carol Wall, "Designing the Program," Education for Changing Unions (Toronto: Between the Lines, 2002), 57.

32. Deborah Barndt, Naming the Moment: Political Analysis for Action (Toronto: Jesuit Center for Social Faith and Justice, 1989).

33. Roberto Antillón Nuñez, Cómo le Hacemos? Para construir conocimiento a través de la sistematización de la práctica social (Guadalajara: IMDEC, 2002).

34. See catalogue of materials for sale at www.imdec.net.

35. Scots educator Liam Kane has produced one of the most comprehensive books on popular education in Latin America: Popular Education and Social Change in Latin America (London: Latin American Bureau, 2001).

36. See www.catalystcenter.ca for a wide range of popular education books, manuals, and tools developed in the Canadian context. See especially Rick Arnold, Bev Burke, Carl James, D'Arcy Martin, and Barb Thomas, Educating for a Change (Toronto: Between the Lines, 1991).

37. Ann Curry-Stevens, "New Forms of Transformative Education: Pedagogy for the Privileged," Journal of Transformative Education 5.1 (January 2007): 33–58.

38. Henry Giroux, Border Crossings: Cultural Workers and the Politics of Education (New York: Routledge, 1992); Ira Shor and Paulo Freire, A Pedagogy for Liberation: Dialogues on Transforming Education (New York: Bergin & Garvey, 1987); Henry Giroux and Roger Simon, Popular Culture: Schooling and Everyday Life (Toronto: Ontario Institute for Studies in Education Press, 1989).

39. Shirley Walters and Lindzi Manicom, Gender in Popular Education: Methods for Empowerment (London: Zed Books, 1996).

40. Barb Thomas and Tina Lopes, Dancing on Live Embers: Challenging Racism in Organizations (Toronto: Between the Lines, 2006); George Dei and Agnes Calliste, Power, Knowledge, and Anti-Racism Education (Halifax: Fernwood Publishing, 2000).

41. Leesa Fawcett, "Bioregional Teaching: How to Climb, Eat, Fall and Learn from Porcupines," Teaching as Activism: Equity Meets Environmentalism, ed. P. Tripp and L. Muzzin (Montreal: McGill-Queens University Press, 2005), 269–280; Leesa Fawcett, "Feral Sociality and (Un)Natural Histories: On Nomadic Ethics and Embodied Learning," Fields of Green: Re-Storying Culture, Environment and Education, ed. M. McKenzie, P. Hart, H. Bai, and B. Jickling (Cresskill, NJ: Hampton Press, 2009), 227–237.

42. Makoto Asano and David Selby, eds., New Century, New Belongings: Essays in Global Education (Tokyo: Nippon Hyoron Sha, 2002).

43. Burke et al., "Designing the Program"; D'Arcy Martin, Thinking Union: Activism and Education in Canada's Labor Movement (Toronto: Between the Lines, 1995).

44. These two quotes from VIVA! partners were taken from preparatory materials submitted prior to our first gathering in 2004.

45. Lisa Campbell-Salazar, a VIVA! intern and research assistant, has pioneered research and social mobilization around mobile activism; see www.mobilerevolutions.org.

46. Deborah Barndt and Amy Shimshon-Santo, "New Tools and Old Contradictions: The VIVA! Project Engages Tekhnologia and New Technology" (paper presented at Latin American Studies Association Congress in Montreal, September 2007).

47. Strega, "The View from the Poststructural Margins," 203.

48. Much of this section has previously appeared in an earlier article: Deborah Barndt, "Touching Minds AND Hearts: Community Arts as Collaborative Research," Handbook of the Arts in Qualitative Research: Perspectives, Methodologies, Examples, and Issues, ed. J. G. Knowles and A. Cole (Thousand Oaks, CA: Sage, 2008), 351–362.

49. Cajete, Look to the Mountain, 146.

50. Ibid., 146.

51. Susan Griffin, The Eros of Everyday Life: Essays on Ecology, Gender and Society (Toronto: Doubleday, 1995).

52. John Berger, Ways of Seeing (London: Penguin Books, 1972).

53. Don Adams and Arlene Goldbard, Community, Culture, and Globalization (New York: Rockefeller Foundation, 2002).

54. Barndt, To Change This House, 18–20.

55. Freire, Pedagogy of the Oppressed.

56. Don Adams and Arlene Goldbard, Creative Community: The Art of Cultural Development (New York: Rockefeller Foundation, 2001).

57. Rose-Avila Magdaleno, "Homegrown Revolution," ColorLines: Race Culture Action (Fall 2003): 10–12.

58. Janine Marchessault, "Reflections on the Dispossessed: Video and the 'Challenge for Change' Experiment," Screen 36.2 (1995): 13–146.

59. Jane Sapp, "To Move and to Change," ARTS: The Arts in Religious and Theological Studies 7.2 (1995): 30–33.

60. See also Kane, Popular Education and Social Change in Latin America; Carlos Nuñez, Educar para Transformar, Transformar para Educar (Guadalajara: IMDEC, 1994).

61. Rick Arnold and Bev Burke, The Popular Education Handbook (Ottawa: Canadian University Service Overseas and Toronto: Ontario Institute for Studies in Education, 1983).

62. Adams and Goldbard, Creative Community, 107.

63. See also Canadian-based websites: www.artbridges.com, www.neighborhoodartsnetwork.org, and www.yorku.ca/cap. The CAN website closed in 2010, but its content can be accessed at http://wayback.archive-it.org/2077/2010090619474/http://www.communityartsnet/.

64. Beverly Naidus, Teaching Outside the Frame: Art for Social Change (Oakland, CA: New Village Press, 2009).

65. Honor Ford-Smith, "Whose Community? Whose Art? The Politics of Reformulating Community Arts," No Frame Around It: Process and Outcome of the A Space Community Art Biennale (Toronto: A Space Gallery, 2001).

66. Ali Starr, "Art and Revolution: Revitalizing Political Protest," Global Uprising: Confronting the Tyrannies of the 21st Century, ed. N. Welton and L. Wolf (Gabriola Island, BC: New Society Publishers, 2002).

67. Maggie Hutcheson, "Demechanizing Our Politics: Street Performance and Making Change," Wild Fire: Art as Activism, ed. D. Barndt (Toronto: Sumach Press, 2006), 79–88.

68. Tom Liacas, "101 Tricks to Play with the Mainstream: Culture Jamming as Subversive Recreation," Autonomous Media: Activating Resistance and Dissent, ed. A. Langlois and F. Dubois (Montreal: Cumulus Press, 2005).

69. Augusto Boal, Games for Actors and Non-Actors, 2nd ed., trans. Adrian Jackson (New York: Routledge, 2002).

70. John Jordan, "The Art of Necessity: The Subversive Imagination of Anti-Road Protest and Reclaim the Streets," Cultural Resistance Reader, ed. S. Duncombe (London: Verso, 2002).

71. Clay Shirky, Here Comes Everybody: The Power of Organizing without Organizations (New York: Penguin Press, 2008).

72. Dorothy Kidd, "Linking Back, Looking Forward," Autonomous Media: Activating Resistance and Dissent, ed. A. Langlois and F. Dubois (Montreal: Cumulus Press, 2005), 151–161.

73. Richard Fung and Monique Kim Gagnon, 13 Conversations about Art and Cultural Race Politics (Montreal: Prendre Parole, 2002).

74. William Cleveland, Mapping the Field: Arts-Based Community Development (http://www.communityarts.net/readingroom/archive/intro-develop.php, 2002), accessed August 3, 2004.

75. See Barndt, To Change This House.

76. Deborah Barndt, "By Whom and for Whom? Intersections of Participatory Research and Community Arts," Provoked by Art: Theorizing Arts-Informed Inquiry, ed. A. Cole, L. Neilsen, J. G. Knowles, T. Luciani (Big Tancook Island, NS: Backalong Books and Center for Arts-Informed Research, OISE, 2004).

77. Stephen de Camois Kemmis, "Critical Education Research," The Canadian Journal for the Study of Adult Education 5 (Winter 1991): 94–119.

78. Susan E. Smith, Dennis K. Williams, and Nancy A Johnson, eds., Nurtured by Knowledge: Learning to Do Participatory Action-Research (New York: Apex Press, 1997).

79. Christine McKenzie, "Popular Communications: Negotiating

Contested Terrain on Nicaragua's Caribbean Coast," unpublished MES paper (Faculty of Environmental Studies, York University, 2002); Ilan Kapoor, "The Devil's in the Theory: A Critical Assessment of Robert Chambers' Work on Participatory Development," Third World Quarterly 23.1 (2002): 101–117.

80. Margaret Kovach, "Emerging from the Margins: Indigenous Methodologies," Research as Resistance: Critical, Indigenous, and Anti-Oppressive Approaches, ed. L. Brown and S. Strega (Toronto: Canadian Scholars' Press / Women's Press, 2005).

81. Colleen Reid, "Advancing Women's Social Justice Agendas: A Feminist Action Research Framework," International Journal of Qualitative Methods 3.3 (2004), retrieved April 10, 2007, from http://www.ualberta.ca/~iiqm/backissues/3_3/html/reid.html.

82. Barndt, "Remapping the Americas," 168–169.

83. Knowles and Cole, eds., Handbook of the Arts in Qualitative Research.

84. Cole, Neilsen, Knowles, eds., Provoked by Art.

85. J. Gary Knowles, Teresa C. Luciani, Ardra L. Cole, and Lorri Neilsen, eds., The Art of Visual Inquiry (Big Tancook Island, NS: Backalong Books and Center for Arts-Informed Research, 2007).

86. J. Gary Knowles, Sara Promislow, and Ardra L. Cole, eds., Creating Scholartistry (Big Tancook Island, NS: Backalong Books and Center for Arts-Informed Research, 2009).

87. Cole and Knowles, "Arts-Informed Research," Handbook of Qualitative Research, 59.

88. Finley, "Arts-Based Research," Handbook of Qualitative Research, 71.

89. Roberto Antillón, Para Construir Conocimiento a través de la Sistematización de la Práctica Social (Guadalajara: IMDEC, 2002).

90. Laura Reinsborough, Sistematización: A Guide to Critical Reflections for Community Art Work (unpublished zine, 2006).

91. Reinsborough and Barndt, "Decolonizing Art, Education and Research in the VIVA! Project," 173.

Introduction to Part I. Recovering Cultural Histories: Engaging Creative Tensions in Indigenous and Diasporic Contexts

1. All the quotations by VIVA! partners used in this chapter are drawn from transcriptions of the VIVA! team gathering in Chiapas, Mexico, in December 2006.

2. Linda Tuhiwai Smith, Decolonizing Methodologies: Research and Indigenous Peoples (New York: Zed Books, 1999), 34.

3. Ibid., 74.

4. Beth Brant, quoted in Thomas King, The Truth About Stories (Toronto: Dead Dog Cafe Productions and CBC, 2003), 144.

Chapter 1. Planting Good Seeds: The Kuna Children's Art Workshops

1. A cold drink made of maize or fruit; it can be either alcoholic, with fermented maize, or nonalcoholic.

2. Thanks to Blas and Evelio Lopez, José Angel Colman, Jorge Ventocilla, and all those who offered testimonies about the process, interviewed by our Canadian collaborator, Laura Reinsborough. Florencio Diaz also helped in preparing this chapter.

3. Jorge Ventocilla, Cacería y subsistencia en Cangandi: Una comunidad de los indígenas Kunas (Hunting and Subsistence in Cangandi: A Community of the Kuna Indigenous People) (Quito: Abya Yala, 1992).

4. All of the quotations used in this chapter are taken from interviews with former staff of the workshops conducted by VIVA! intern Laura Reinsborough in Panama, August 2005.

5. Simon Bolivar was a liberator of Latin America in the struggle for independence from Spain.

6. Instituto Nacional de Estadística y Censo de Panamá, http://www.contraloria.gob.pa/inec/.

7. Community town criers and police who maintain security in the community and who invite the community members to the meetings.

8. Influential community leaders who offer analysis of the issues to clarify them before making decisions.

9. The Tule Revolution of 1925 was a popular revolt of the Kuna people against the Panamanian government, through which they gained cultural autonomy.

10. Jorge Ventocilla, "Devolviendo la información a las comunidades: experiencias con los Kunas" (Returning the information to the communities: experiences with the Kunas) (Panama City: Smithsonian Institution).

Chapter 2. The Lost Body: Recovering Memory— A Personal Legacy

Sections of this chapter have appeared earlier in Diane Roberts, "Women, Art and Community Activism," Women and Environments International 72–73 (December 2006): 25–27.

1. Hervé Maxi and Zab Maboungou dance classes held at Compagnie Danse Nyata-Nyata, Montreal, Quebec. www.nyata-nyata.org.

2. http://nobelprize.org/nobel-prizes/literature/laureates/1992/walcott-lecture.htm.

3. Langston Hughes's poem "The Negro Speaks of Rivers," discussed in James Baldwin, "Sermons and Blues," The New York Times Book Review (March 29, 1959), 6.

4. Maya Angelou, Still I Rise (New York: Random House, 1978).

5. Taken from a proposal submitted by Heather Hermant and Di-

ane Roberts to Toronto Harbourfront Center's Fresh Ground Arts Series, Toronto, Canada.

6. Ibid.

7. Ibid.

8. Gloria Anzaldua, Borderlands / La Frontera: The New Mestiza (Berkeley: Quinto Sol Publications, 1973), 237.

9. New World African spiritual practices derived from Yoruban spiritual practice that often involves ritual possession.

Introduction to Part II. Transforming Urban Spaces: From Postcolonial Neighborhoods to Public Squares

1. The spiral can found in many ancestral practices of diverse origins; consider, for example, the Celtic tri-spiral, which can be traced back to the Druids in what is now known as the United Kingdom. Of political significance to VIVA! partners, however, is the fact that the spiral also echoes the Zapatista symbol of the caracol, referring simultaneously to the conch shell that was a major form of popular communications among Indigenous peoples in Chiapas and the snail shell (which we have adopted as a symbol). The caracol is the name given to the seat of autonomous government established by the Zapatistas in the liberated zones of Chiapas, Mexico.

2. City of Toronto website, http://www.toronto.ca/toronto_facts/diversity.htm.

3. Maggie Hutcheson, Dissertation Proposal (Faculty of Environmental Studies, York University, March 2010), 3.

4. Richard Florida, The Rise of the Creative Class: And How It's Transforming Work, Leisure, and Everyday Life (New York: Basic Books, 2003).

5. Jane M. Jacobs, Edge of Empire: Postcolonialism and the City (New York: Routledge, 1996), 4.

Chapter 3. Out of the Tunnel There Came Tea: Jumblies Theatre's Bridge of One Hair Project

This chapter was prepared with commentary from collaborating artists Loree Lawrence, Noah Kenneally, Leah Houston and Catherine Campbell in 2006, with postscripts from 2007 and 2008.

1. For information on the community play movement, the ongoing work of Jumblies Theatre, and the Bridge of One Hair project, including videos, articles, and references, please contact us at: info@jumbliestheatre.org or www.jumbliestheatre.org.

2. Dictionary definition of "tension."

3. Duke Redbird. Old Woman. Transcribed by Ruth Howard from a CD recording given her by Redbird when he offered the poem for the

performance, 2007.

4. Hawa Jibril, "I Had a Dream," The Poetry and the Times of Hawa Jibril, ed. and trans. Faduma Ahmed Alim (Toronto: Jumblies Press, 2008), adapted for "Bridge of One Hair" by Ruth Howard.

5. http://www.nonsenselit.org/Lear/ns/jumblies.html.

Chapter 4. Telling Our Stories: Training Artists to Engage with Communities

1. "First Nations" is used to recognize the distinct nations of peoples who lived on the land before it was colonized by Europeans and called Canada.

2. City of Toronto website. By 2031, it is projected that 67 percent of Toronto's population will be composed of minorities.

3. "Flashforward: Projecting Population and Employment to 2031 in a Mature Urban Area" on our Toronto Plan pages. http://www.toronto.ca/torontoplan/pdf/flash_sec1A.pdf.

4. Paulo Freire, Pedagogy of the Oppressed (New York: Continuum, 1970).

5. For the Catalyst Centre mission statement and popular education resources, see www.catalystcentre.ca.

6. Sherene Razack, "Storytelling for Social Change," Looking White People in the Eye: Gender, Race, and Culture in Courtrooms and Classrooms (Toronto: University of Toronto Press, 1998), 3–55.

7. Bev Burke, Jojo Geronimo, D'Arcy Martin, Barb Thomas, and Carol Wall, eds., Education for Changing Unions (Toronto: Between the Lines, 2003). For further explanation of the spiral model, see Burke et al., eds., Educating for a Change, 38.

8. Darren O'Donnell, Social Acupuncture: A Guide to Suicide, Performance and Utopia (Toronto: Coach House Books, 2006), 30.

9. Antonio Gramsci coined the term "hegemony," which refers to the dominant ideology of a time. Gramsci explained that dominant discourses or beliefs can be inscribed and upheld by force. However, more often people are enticed into subscribing to dominant values and ideals as a result of messages they receive and accept through mediums such as educational institutions, popular culture, and the media. See Antonio Gramsci, Selections from the Prison Notebooks, ed. Quintin Hoare and Geoffrey-Nowell Smith, (New York: International, 1971).

Chapter 5. A Melting Pot Where Diverse Lives Converge: Tianguis Cultural de Guadalajara

1. Unfortunately, among the most contemporary tianguis, it has become common to sell a wide range of imported products, mainly from China, at low prices but also of poor quality. Traditional music has been replaced by stereos playing loud, outrageous music of all kinds. The

sale of pirate products is another controversial point. Due to the underground economy, merchants at the tianguis find themselves in conflict with merchants at established businesses.

2. Mexican Institute for Community Development, A.C. (IMDEC) is an NGO with more than forty years of work in popular education and communication. It has a strong presence at the local and national as well as the Latin American level. IMDEC has supported the process of Tianguis Cultural of Guadalajara since its beginnings through a relationship of mutual friendship and support. The institute invited Tianguis to collaborate with them on the VIVA! project and to share the experience of the international exchange.

Introduction to Part III. Community-University Collaborations: Blurring the Boundaries

1. See www.communitybasedresearch.ca; http://web.uvic.ca/ocbr/.

2. Since the 1990s, for example, the Social Science and Humanities Research Council has funded multipartnered collaborative projects through the Community University Research Alliance (CURA) program and Partnership Grants.

3. Internationalizing of universities is often driven more by economic motives (e.g., amassing exorbitant student fees from elite international students or partnering with banks to train managers in third world branches) than by an openness to collaboration across different kinds of knowledges and ways of knowing. See Deborah Barndt, "Reframing Internationalization in a (Post)Colonial and Diasporic Context: Two Initiatives at York University," Canada's Universities Go Global, ed. Roopa Trilokekar, Glen Jones, and Adrian Shubert (Toronto: James Lorimer and Company, 2009).

4. Marina Niks, "The Politics of Collaborative Research between University-Based and Non-University-Based Researchers," unpublished PhD diss. (Vancouver, BC: University of British Columbia, 2004).

Chapter 6. Painting by Listening: Participatory Community Mural Production

1. http://mapserver.inegi.gob.mx/geografia/espanol/datosgeogra/extterri/frontera.cfm?c=154, accessed October 2006.

2. Mexico's Present Profile http://www.campus-oei.org/cultura/mexico/c3.htm, accessed October 2006.

3. Comisión Nacional para el Desarrollo de los Pueblos Indígenas (CDI), "Lenguas indígenas: Diversidad etnolingüística," paragraphs 3 and 5. http://es.wikipedia.org/wiki/Pueblos_indígenas_de_México http://cdi.gob.mx/index.php?id_seccion=90, accessed October 2006.

4. National Association of Universities and Higher Education Institutions (ANUIES), http://www.anuies.mx/la_anuies/afiliadas.php http://www.anuies.mx/la_anuies/diries/, accessed October 2006.

5. The fundamental assumption that guides the organization of the units within the Xochimilco campus, the teaching methodology, and the activities of the university toward social change has three objectives:
• To relate the teaching-learning process with real socially defined problems;
• To break with traditional teaching models, and to establish a new methodology; in which the student would be the "designer of his (her) own learning process";
• To establish the teaching/research/service triad as the axis of the teaching-learning process.

Origen y Misión de la UAM-Xochimilco, http//www.xoc,uam/identidad/modelo.html, accessed October 2006.

6. One of the basic concepts still to be clarified is "community." Maybe because of its lofty connotation, its use has been widespread to define all kinds of social groups. In the beginning, our project was based on the concept of a geographic or "face-to-face community." This is typical of the ancient cultures that still survive thanks to that particular organization process. The word "community," as used by a great number of thinkers over the past two centuries, includes all forms of relationships, characterized by a high degree of intimacy, emotional depth, moral commitment, social grouping, and length of existence. The community is based on the human being conceived as a whole, not according to any role she or he may play within a social organization. Its psychological strength comes from more profound levels of motivation than mere interest, and it is completed by giving up the individual will, a situation impossible within associations led by mere convenience or rational sense. A community is a fusion of feeling and thought, of tradition and commitment, of belonging and will. See Robert Nisbet, La formación del pensamiento sociológico, 1 (Buenos Aires: Amorrortu, 1990), 71–72.

7. Doña Olga, participant in the mural Metamorfosis (Metamorphosis), San Miguel Ajusco, Mexico, 2003.

8. Miguel, a participant in the mural Los Hijos del Maíz, Oventic, Chiapas. 2001.

9. Manuel, a teaching promotor or facilitator at the ESRAZ and participant in the mural Los Hijos del Maíz, Oventic, Chiapas. 2001.

10. Hate, a participant in the mural at San Miguel Ajusco, Mexico, 2001.

11. Alexandra, a participant in the mural Un mundo donde quepan muchos mundos in Munich, Germany, 2001.

12. To diminish conflicts between ideas, we try to suspend judgment (to avoid negative judgments) during the brainstorming process, while we are generating ideas. On the contrary, we stimulate the expression of all kinds of ideas, we avoid interruptions and "destructive" comments such as "that is so exaggerated," "we won't be able to do it," or "that'll need a lot of money." Once the ideas are well identified and organized, we take time for collective appreciation and reflection, to

facilitate the integration and expression of ideas (positive judgment).

13. Rosalía Aida Hernández (CIESAS) and Héctor Ortiz Elizondo (UAM-I), "Diferentes pero Iguales: Los pueblos indígenas en México y el acceso a la justicia," Conference at the Center for U.S.-Mexican Studies, May 2003. http://repositories.cdlib.org/cgi/viewcontent.cgi?article=1035&context=usmex.

Chapter 7. Connecting the Dots: Linking Schools and Universities through the Arts

1. For more information, see Lawrence B. Graaf, Kevin Mulroy, Quintard Taylor, Seeking El Dorado: African Americans in California (Seattle: University of Washington Press, 2001).

2. Los Angeles is a landscape of ethnic and economic enclaves. In Los Angeles, one will find a vital "Chinatown," "Thai Town," "Historic Filipino Town," "Korea Town," "Little India," "Little Armenia," "Little Ethiopia," and many more. These ethnogeographical designations suggest alternative cultural maps, and are a strategy that has been used for communities to claim space and make Los Angeles feel more like home.

3. See Richard Valencia, The Mexican American Struggle for Equal Educational Opportunity in Mendez v. Westminster: Helping to Pave the Way for Brown v. Board of Education (Malden, MA: Blackwell, 2005).

4. The University of California is a public university that is a part of a multi-tiered system of public higher education in California that includes a network of community colleges and California State Universities.

5. Thomas Turner, Los Angeles, correspondence with author, 23 April, 2007.

6. For more information, see Amy Shimshon-Santo, "Arts Impact: Lessons from ArtsBridge," Journal for Teaching Through the Arts 6, 1 (2010), www.escholarship.org/uc/item/8je1p385#page-1.

7. Cynthia Wennstrom, Los Angeles, poetry assignment for ArtsBridge course, March 2, 2007.

8. Tameka Norris, written reflection for ArtsBridge course assignment, March 2008.

9. "Dropouts by Ethnic Designation by Grade," Los Angeles Unified School District for the Year 2007–2008, California Department of Education, Educational Demographics Office, prepared March 16, 2010.

10. Tameka Norris, written reflection, March 2008.

11. "Exercise My Rights," www.titleix.info, accessed March 16, 2010,

12. Norm Lacy, Santa Monica, correspondence with author, March 9, 2006.

13. Desiree Gallardo, Los Angeles, online blog, March 8, 2007.

14. Sonia Balonas, personal interview with author, Los Angeles, July 14, 2006.

15. A quinceañera is a traditional rite of passage ceremony that recognizes the transition from girlhood into womanhood. Its name in Spanish is drawn from the age at which it is usually performed, when a person is quince or fifteen years old.

16. Kris Gutierrez and Marjorie Orellana, "At Last: What's the Problem? Constructing Different Genres for the Study of English Learners," Research in the Teaching of English (RTE) 41.1 (2006): 19.

17. Oscar Neal, public testimony at ArtsBridge citywide public gathering, Los Angeles, March 17, 2006.

Epilogue: Critical Hope

1. Raúl Leis, secretary general of the Latin American Council for Adult Education (CEAAL), used this phrase at the VIVA! gathering in Achiote, Panama, in August 2005.

2. For further information, see the website of the Community Arts Practice (CAP) program at York University: www.yorku.ca/cap.

3. http://vpacademic.yorku.ca/whitepaper/, accessed June 30, 2010.

4. Martha Nussbaum quoted in John Allemang, "Socrates Would Be So Proud," The Globe and Mail, June 11, 2010, F1.

Glossary

1. Michel Foucault, "Nietzsche, Genealogy, History," The Essential Foucault, ed. Paul Rabinow and Nikolas Rose (New York: New Press, 2003), 351–369.

2. Raymond Williams, Keywords: A Vocabulary of Culture and Society (London: Fontana, 1976); and New Keywords: A Revised Vocabulary of Culture and Society, ed. Tony Bennett, Lawrence Grossberg, and Meaghan Morris (Oxford, UK: Blackwell, 2005).

Glossary

Janna Gorham and Deborah Barndt

This glossary attempts to explain some of the key terms found in this book. However, we caution against taking any of these as firm or fixed definitions. We would have preferred to construct a genealogy,[1] tracing the shifting and even contradictory meanings of these concepts from one place and time to another; a genealogical approach contends that language cannot be understood in isolation from the contexts or ecologies from which they arise. Just as education is not neutral, neither are words, especially what Raymond Williams coined as "key words,"[2] which reflect political and philosophical struggles. We emphasize here the specific interpretation of these concepts in the VIVA! project, and encourage readers to consider the multiple and potential meanings of these words in their own contexts and to engage in ongoing discussions about their ideological implications.

Aesthetics: A central issue in community arts, ranging from philosophical evaluations of what is beautiful (e.g., classical Western approaches that "universalize" the criteria for worthy art and privilege the individual as artist) to other traditions and culturally diverse aesthetics, such as those that consider the aesthetic and spiritual to be intertwined.

Alternative media: A strategic challenge to mass media outlets (dominated by corporate interests) to raise the visibility of diverse perspectives for social and political change and to serve the interests of communities.

Antiracism: Form of political action to combat structural racism and oppression reproduced through historically constructed political, economic, and social institutions. An antiracist perspective affirms different epistemologies, or ways of knowing, and intercultural leadership among youth and adults. It also aims to get White people to acknowledge their own privilege, to become allies, and to work for anti-racist social change.

Arts-based and arts-informed research: These models explore alternative processes and representational forms in academic discourse—constructing a different path through art by combining inquiry, social engagement, and community activism.

Autonomous community or region: Refers to an area where Indigenous and historically marginalized populations are reclaiming land and their own governance structures and processes; among VIVA! projects, for example, BilwiVision strengthens the autonomous region of the Nicaraguan Caribbean Coast and Painting by Listening reinforces Indigenous self-determination in Zapatista autonomous zones.

Collaboration: A central principle and practice in community arts, referring to different levels of working together creatively: from artists collaborating with each other and with grassroots groups, to collaboration among community members as they develop their own artistic practice.

Colonization: Referring to the historical process of the occupation of land and genocide of Indigenous peoples and nations in Latin America, Asia, and Africa by European nations beginning in the sixteenth century, and continuing in multiple forms in the present.

Community arts: Encompassing a wide range of practices and traditions, it engages people in representing their collective identities, histories, and aspirations in multiple forms of expression. For VIVA!, it involves reclaiming the right and capacity of everyone to express themselves through their own cultural and hybrid forms.

Community-based research: This collaborative research acknowledges historical inequities between communities and universities and promotes community-based knowledge production processes for a richer and more socially useful understanding of the world around us. In the VIVA! project it entails partnering locally and transnationally to collectively produce knowledge and to share the results of locally grounded participatory action research across distinct contexts.

Community cultural development: A range of cultural capacity-building practices undertaken by artists who collaborate with community members to express themselves through arts and communications media, while working toward social change. Distinguished from more conservative and "top-down" forms of arts dissemination.

Conjunctural analysis: An approach to analyzing the interrelation and balance of forces (political, economic, ideological) at play in any particular moment in time; coupled with structural analysis, conjunctural analysis aims to identify the specific free space that the moment offers to act strategically to forward processes of structural change.

Conscientization: Coined by Brazilian educator Paulo Freire, *concientización* is the popular education process through which individuals situate their personal experiences in larger social structures, identify their common ground, and work collectively to change the oppressive conditions of their lives.

Counter-hegemony: Resistance and struggle for change among marginalized peoples in the cultural sphere: by challenging and transforming dominant hegemony, popular education and community arts are approaches to developing critical social consciousness and collective action.

Creative tensions: The strains and challenges arising in community-based art practices that create points of resistance between issues of process/product, aesthetics/ethics, cultural reclamation / cultural reinvention, spiritual/political, and body/earth but offer opportunities for reflection and dialogue.

Critical hope: A dialectical notion that integrates critical social analysis with the creative imagination of the possibilities that exist within the constraints of any situation; a belief in people's capacities to understand the root causes of oppressive conditions of their lives while not being paralyzed by analysis but rather empowered to work to change them.

Critical thinking: Conscious and mindful questioning that engages more senses than logic alone: in education, the cultivation of self-examination, empathy, and a capacity for contextualizing knowledge in a historical process. By politicizing social issues within historical and cultural contexts, it challenges broad generalizations of "truth" and meaning (e.g., problematizes notions of "objectivity" in research).

Cultural reclamation: An active and transformative process in which lost, stolen, or buried legacies are sought after and pieced together again—often in art-making practices that encourage multiple cultural expressions and ways of knowing.

Cultural reinvention: A more complex understanding of historical and cultural reclamation as an active process that engages in a constant reenvisioning of culture to create hybrid practices.

Decolonization: Comprises several interrelated processes: acknowledging the history of colonialism; working to undo the effects of colonialism; striving to unlearn habits, attitudes, and behaviors that continue to perpetuate colonialism; and challenging and transforming institutional manifestations of colonialism.

Dialogue: Central to the popular education theory of Paulo Freire, refers to a deep conversation based on respect, openness, and a willingness to be transformed; in Personal Legacy work it is the dynamic relationship between subject, performer, facilitator, and witness.

Diaspora: Populations that have been uprooted from their countries of origin by slavery, genocide, war, economic migration, indentured labor or political exile, and scattered across the globe in communities where they are assimilated and/or fight to maintain their cultures, often in the face of institutional discrimination and racism.

Diasporic: Refers to the movement, migration, and/or displacement of populations from common territory and shared heritage, ethnicity, or cultural origin as well as processes through which groups claim and create multiple and diverse identities.

Diversity: Referring often to racial and ethnocultural diversity; in the Canadian context another expression for the "mosaic multiculturalism" agenda that privileges a dominant cultural norm and gaze, marginalizes other traditions, and forces assimilation.

Dualistic thinking: An approach or belief that divides the universe into polar oppositions (based on Enlightenment thought), which may be reflected in social discourse, language, or action and limits one's ability to accept more complex, dynamic, and nuanced understandings of the world.

Embodied knowing and learning: Emphasizes and reclaims the body's experiential knowledge(s) by challenging a mind/body split, which derives from Eurocentric and/or colonial frameworks: unlike Indigenous cosmovisions that are rooted in the interconnectedness of bodies and other living entities.

Environmental education: A field of pedagogy that aims to educate people about, for, and with the environment, often promoting a reconnection between human and more than human beings; a critical approach to environmental education connects the historical domination of nature with the domination of other marginalized peoples (Indigenous, Third World, and women).

Epistemology: A perspective on how we know what we know; examines the production of knowledge(s) and its breadth and limitations by posing questions about how truth, belief, and "reason" shape knowledge structures.

Ethics: The principles upon which the content and process of art-making are established to foster a vision and practice that serves, responds to, expresses, and engages communities in a just, conscious, and responsible manner.

Eurocentricism: A legacy of perspectives that assume European-derived civilizations, peoples, and histories are superior to non-Western cultures and that don't acknowledge how European colonialism continues to inform capitalist modernity, culture, language, and art.

Facilitator: The role taken by the educator/researcher/artist who nurtures a process of participatory research, collective knowledge production, and collaborative artistic creation, tapping and developing the knowledges, skills, and resources of participants; contrasts with authoritarian and elitist notions of the teacher, researcher, or artist.

Formal, nonformal, and informal learning: Formal learning involves institutionalized curricula in educational establishments; nonformal learning may be semistructured but outside of formal education; informal learning happens through all daily interactions.

Hegemony: As articulated by Antonio Gramsci, power is considered relational, or persuasion from above as well as consent from below. A form of ideological control through intellectual and moral persuasion, manifested in cultural forms such as art, media, education, and religion.

Identity: One's conceptualization of selfhood as well as an experience that is part of a greater whole or group. The notion of cultural homogeneity or pure/unchanging identity has been contested and in community arts people may represent collective identities in multiple ways that reflect transformative perspectives of history, culture, heritage, and belonging.

Indigenous: Original habitants in a land and deeply culturally connected to it, often resisting colonization, neoliberal globalization, and cultural imperialism; in Latin America, the term "Indigenous" is more common, while in Canada, "First Nations" or "Aboriginals" prevail, and in the United States, "Indian" or "Native" are used (all contested and politically charged terms).

Media literacy: A method of cultivating cultural literacy in arts by supporting critical analysis of media, language development, and design/ visual arts / software skills to foster public participation, build community, encourage cultural reclamation, and transform institutions.

Neoliberal corporate globalization: The process whereby multinational corporations exercise unbridled political power and trade through the deregulation of financial markets, which harm the health and livelihood of workers, local economies, and the environment. In contrast, a globalizing civil society emerging from a movement of Indigenous peoples, communities of color, and their allies can challenge Eurocentric values and dominant discourse within corporate media.

Participatory action research: A form of critical, libratory research in which groups identify the issues to be studied, participate in the data gathering and analysis, take action, and reflect on that action. Has been critiqued by postcolonial, feminist, and critical development scholars for potentially perpetuating colonial relations while also taken up by Indigenous researchers for its relational qualities and emancipatory methods.

Personal Legacy: A theatrical practice that uses the emotional, spiritual, physical, and intellectual aspects of self and delves into participants' ancestral histories: stemming from the context of the colonized body but also encouraging participants of various backgrounds and arts disciplines to use their lives as sources of creativity and means for understanding others.

Popular communications: Democratization of art and media through both the critical and creative processes to understand root causes of oppression and imagine means for change. Commonly used in Latin American contexts, it refers to collective inquiry and knowledge dissemination to/with poor majorities (e.g., community radio, popular theatre, *nueva cancion* or new song, and video).

Popular education: A practice developed largely in Latin America that uncovers and challenges power relations inherent in education by drawing upon and revaluing the experiences and perceptions of learners: making the learner-teacher relationship reciprocal and linking links collective analysis to action for social change.

Postcolonial theory: An umbrella term for analyses that examine colonialism's legacy, including recognizing that assumptions underlying the logic of colonialism continue to be active forces with social, cultural, political, and material implications; postcolonial theory makes space for multiple voices, particularly those silenced by dominant discourses.

Praxis: A cultivated awareness of one's condition and shared experiences: both reflecting and acting upon the world to enact social change; the dynamic interaction of active contemplation and reflective practice.

Self-reflexivity: A "bending back" on self as one reflects upon the ways one is shaped by forces or social structures, which can lead to a better understanding of one's social location, its limitations and possibilities.

Sistematización: A participatory process developed by Central American popular educators to involve a group in systematically revisiting its practice in order to find its deeper meaning and to inform future actions; similar to participatory action research.

Social communications: A form of cultural resistance that encourages communities to identify their own qualities and needs, as well as their social, spiritual, and political aspirations by developing community-based artistic expression as means of dialogue, building solidarity, and strengthening a group's recognition of its cultural, social, and political identity.

Social justice: A way of engaging communities to name and address apparent and unacknowledged forms of oppression such as racism, violence, and silencing, which is, at its core, about demonstrating the empowerment of people: often grounded in collective practices and community development that resist unjust uses of power.

Spirituality: Multiple spiritual traditions are recognized as integral threads of community art-making, particularly in Indigenous and diasporic contexts where the ritual dimensions of creative processes engage the hearts, minds, and spirits of those involved.

Tianguis Cultural: *Tianguis* is the Nahuat word for "marketplace"; the youth-driven cultural marketplace in Guadalajara, Mexico, honors the Indigenous roots of their alternative public space emphasizing the exchange of multiple forms of cultural production and expression.

About the Editor, Contributors, and Videographers

Editor

DEBORAH BARNDT is a popular educator, photographer, and professor in the faculty of environmental studies at York University in Toronto, Canada. Initiator of the VIVA! project, she also coordinates the Community Arts Practice program at York; she has exhibited her photos widely and published over ten books, about popular education, community arts, food, gender, and globalization.

Contributors

JESÚS ALEMANCIA is the director of CEASPA in Panama, where he coordinates development, environment, and human rights projects with Indigenous organizations. As a sociologist and Kuna, he has contributed to the recovery of Kuna oral history and to an analysis of Kuna autonomy and sociocultural changes due to migration, education, and economic investments in Kuna Yala.

LEONARDO DAVID DE ANDA GONZALEZ is a founder of Tianguis Cultural in Guadalajara, Mexico, and served as its president for six years. He also founded the Black Sheep Project and Ultraviolet Publications, through which he has mounted installations and written and designed various books, most recently *Lotería Tianguis Cultural*, with photos honoring the countercultural work of the project featured in this book.

MARGARITA ANTONIO is a Miskitu journalist, an activist in regional Indigenous women's networks, and serves as a UNESCO Officer on the Caribbean Coast of Nicaragua. Founder of the Institute for Intercultural Communication of URACCAN, she promoted BilwiVision, the community television program, and co-organized the Fourth Encounter of the VIVA! project in Nicaragua in 2010.

REYNA ARMIDA DUARTE coordinated the production team of BilwiVision, the community television station of URACCAN on the Caribbean Coast of Nicaragua until 2010, promoting communications across ethnic divides. A seasoned journalist, she is currently working with the municipal Commission for Children, Youth, and Women, aiming to reduce domestic violence; she integrates popular communications into this advocacy work.

JANNA GORHAM is an artist, student, and group facilitator for children with developmental disabilities. During her MA in Critical Disability Studies, she focused on trauma, memory, and embodied heritage(s) and is now exploring the therapeutic dimensions of community arts through both the Community Arts Practice (CAP) program at York University and the Ontario College of Art and Design.

RUTH HOWARD is a theatre designer and creator, and the founder and artistic director of Jumblies Theatre, a Toronto-based company that creates large-scale arts and theatre projects with diverse communities through long-term residencies. She created and produced award-winning community play productions in four Toronto neighborhoods, has nurtured the development of two off-shoot organizations, and has developed Jumblies Studio, offering mentorship to emerging community artists.

SERGIO EDUARDO (LALO) MARTÍNEZ MAYORAL is an active member of Tianguis Cultural in Guadalajara, Mexico, and has contributed his skills as a graphic designer and musician, as an organizer of cultural events and free speech forums, and as an exhibitor of socially critical photography. He founded his own integrated graphic design agency and is president of the Arlekin Collective, a group of socially committed artists, photographers, and illustrators.

CHRISTINE MCKENZIE worked at the Catalyst Centre as a popular educator when she coordinated the train-the-trainer project in Toronto, Canada. She has worked with social justice, women's and human rights groups across Canada and Central America. She recently completed a PhD in adult education at the Ontario Institute for Studies in Education, focusing on understanding the ways feminists facilitate consciousness raising around identity, power, and oppression with differently located women in noncredit educational contexts.

DIANE ROBERTS is a Caribbean Canadian theatre artist working from an Africentric perspective, which has informed the development of the Personal Legacy project and the Arrivals project in the past five years. She is currently artistic director of urban ink productions, which develops and produces aboriginal and diverse cultural works of theatre, writing, and film, integrating artistic disciplines and bringing together different cultural and artistic perspectives and interracial experiences.

SERGIO G. (CHECO) VALDEZ RUVALCABA teaches drawing, group process, and creativity in the Social Communications Department at the Metropolitan Autonomous University in Mexico City. He has exhibited widely and has trained many people in participatory community mural production throughout Mexico and internationally. In recent years, this has resulted in more than forty murals in Indigenous communities in Chiapas, Mexico.

The Painting by Listening process has been the subject of many studies, videos, and conferences.

AMY SHIMSHON-SANTO is a Los Angeles–based performing artist, educator, and researcher. As ArtsBridge director for UCLA's School for the Arts and Architecture, she prepared arts educators, built arts education infrastructure, and cultivated K–12 community partnerships. She recently edited *Art = Education: Connecting Learning Communities in Los Angeles* (University of California Press), and has published poetry and short stories in addition to social research on arts education, urban schooling, and community development.

Videographers

LORETO BRAVO is an independent media producer working out of Mexico and active transnationally. She helped to mount the website of the VIVA! project and produced videos on the Painting by Listening project in Mexico as well as the Telling Our Stories project in Toronto, Canada, as part of an international exchange.

LISA CAMPBELL-SALAZAR worked as a York University graduate student on the VIVA! project book, DVD, and website, collaborating onsite with a number of the partner organizations including UCLA ArtsBridge in Los Angeles and the Latin American Council for Adult Education in Panama. Currently she coordinates the TRIP! project, a youth-led harm reduction media project run out of Central Toronto Community Health Centers.

JUAN JOSÉ (PATO) ESQUIVEL has worked for two decades as a popular educator and video producer with the Mexican Institute for Community Development (IMDEC) in Guadalajara, Mexico, where he also co-coordinated the VIVA! video productions. Pato is a leader in popular communications in Central American networks and is currently working on environmental projects in rural Jalisco.

HEATHER HERMANT participated in the VIVA! project as an intern with Painting by Listening; as Diane Roberts's key collaborator on Personal Legacy; and as co-videographer/editor on the Painting by Listening and Personal Legacy videos. Heather's one-woman show developed through Personal Legacy, *ribcage: this wide passage*, premiered in Vancouver in April 2010. A spoken-word, theatre, and installation artist, she has taught in York University's Community Arts Practice certificate in Toronto since 2005.

MAGGIE HUTCHESON participated in the VIVA! project from its very beginning, as a researcher, conference organizer, and co-coordinator of the VIVA! video productions. She produced, directed, and edited the overview video as well as the Jumblies Theatre video. Maggie is currently a PhD candidate in environmental studies at York University, where her work focuses on the presentation of contested histories through site-specific art; she also teaches in the Community Arts Practice program.

LAURA REINSBOROUGH is a community artist and organizer, who worked on the VIVA! project as an intern with CEASPA in Panama, as a conference organizer, and as a videographer. After completing her master's in Environmental Studies, she worked with the Arts Access program of the Art Gallery of Ontario and founded a local food initiative, Not Far from the Tree, which she coordinates.

Contacts for VIVA! Project Partner Organizations

Coordination

Faculty of Environmental Studies, York University, 4700 Keele Street, Toronto, Ontario M3J 1P3
www.yorku.ca/fes, www.yorku.ca/cap
Deborah Barndt, coordinator, dbarndt@yorku.ca
Research assistants and videographers:
Lisa Campbell, lisa@mobilerevolutions.org
Heather Hermant, heatherhermant@gmail.com
Maggie Hutcheson, mhutch@yorku.ca
Laura Reinsborough, laura.reinsborough@gmail.com

University Partners

Universidad de las Regiones Autónomas de la Costa Caribe Nicaragüense (URACCAN), Bilwi, RAAN, Nicaragua
www.uraccan.edu.ni
Margarita Antonio, antoniomargarita@yahoo.com.mx
Aracelly Duarte, ingwanka64@yahoo.com
University of California, Los Angeles

ArtsBridge program, School of Art and Architecture
http://www.arts.ucla.edu/artsbridge
http://www.artsbridgeamerica.com
Amy Shimshon-Santo, former director, shimshona4@gmail.com

Universidad Autónoma Metropolitana (UAM), Social Communications Department, Mexico City, Mexico
Sergio Valdez Ruvalcaba (Checo Valdez)
pintarobedeciendo@gmail.com

Community Partners

Catalyst Centre
575 Palmerson Avenue, Toronto, Ontario M6G 2P6
www.catalystcenter.ca, info@catalystcenter.ca
Christine McKenzie, former member, c-mckenzie@sympatico.ca
Jin Huh, former member, jin@riseup.net

CEASPA, Centro de Estudios y Acción Social Panameño, Vía Cincuentenario,
No. 84, Coco del Mar, San Francisco, Panamá
Apartado Postal: 0819-10043
www.ceaspa.org.pa, ceaspa@cwpanama.net
Jesús Alemancia, director, jaleman@hotmail.co
José Angel Colman, begipinsae@hotmail.com

IMDEC, Instituto Mexicano para el Desarrollo Comunitario
Pino 2237, Col. Del Fresno
C.P. 44900 Guadalajara, Jalisco, Mexico

Juan José (Pato) Esquivel, patoesquivel@gmail.com
imdec@laneta.apc.org

Tianguis Cultural
Sergio Eduardo Mayoral Martínez, eddigma@gmail.com
Leonardo David de Anda Gonzalez, tianguiscultural@yahoo.com.mx

Jumblies Theatre, www.jumbliestheatre.org
Toronto, Ontario, Canada
Ruth Howard, artistic director, ruth@jumbliestheatre.org

The Personal Legacy project, urban ink productions
PO Box 2404, Stn. Terminal
Vancouver, British Columbia, V6B 3W7
www.urbanink.ca, info@urbanink.ca
Diane Roberts, artistic director, dirobe@urbanink.ca
Heather Hermant, heatherhermant@gmail.com

Photo and Drawing Credits

Cover photograph: Deborah Barndt.

Frontmatter: Deborah Barndt, i, iii; iv; Katherine Fleitas, ii; Christine McKenzie, v.

Preface: Margie Adam/ArtWork, viii; Loreto Bravo, x; Deborah Barndt, ix, xi, xii, xiii, xiv.

Acknowledgments: Amanda Montgomery, xvi (top left); Heather Hermant, xvi (top right); Gerardo Rodriguez, xvi (bottom right); Deborah Barndt, xviii; xix; xx.

Introduction: Rooted in Place, Politics, Passion and Praxis: All photos by Deborah Barndt, except Heather Hermant, 11; Drawing by Margie Adam/Artwork, 1.

Introduction to Section 1: Deborah Barndt, 20, 21, 24, 25, 27; Collectiv de Solidaritat amb la Rebellió Zapatista de Barcelona, 23.

Chapter 1. Planting Good Seeds: Kuna Children's Art Workshop archives, 31, 35; Deborah Barndt, 30, 32, 33, 34, 37, 38, 41.

Chapter 2. The Lost Body: Heather Hermant, 42, 45, 51; Maggie Hutcheson, 47; Claude Latour, 48; Simon Rossiter, 52; Diane Roberts, 50, 54.

Introduction to Section 2: Drawings by Margie Adam/ArtWork; photos by Deborah Barndt.

Chapter 3. Out of the Tunnel There Came Tea: Deborah Barndt, 61, both images, 64, 66, 69, 71; Katherine Fleitas, 63, 65, 67, 68, 70, 72.

Chapter 4. Telling Our Stories: Deborah Barndt, 75; Margie Adam/ArtWork (courtesy of Between the Lines), 78; Courtesy of Christine McKenzie, 79, 80, 81a; Mario del Monte Martinez, 81b; Darren O'Donnell, 83.

Chapter 5. A Melting Pot Where Lives Converge: All photos by Deborah Barndt.

Introduction to Section 3: Permission of Checo Valdez, 100.

Chapter 6. Painting by Listening: Checo Valdez, 102, 104, 109, 110; Heather Hermant, 106, 107, 108; Gerardo Marván Enriques, 112.

Chapter 7. Connecting the Dots: Joyce Lin, 115, 119, 122; Amy Shimshon-Santo, 113, 115, 117, 120, 122, 123; Amitis Motavelli, 118.

Chapter 8. With Our Images, Voices, and Cultures: All photos by Deborah Barndt.

Epilogue: Critical Hope: Errol Young, 133; Monique Mojica, 135; Deborah Barndt, 136.

¡VIVA!

Community Arts and Popular Education in the Americas

A DVD with nine bilingual videos

The DVD accompanying this book includes the following nine bilingual videos that correspond with the chapters; the first video offers an overview of the VIVA! project presented in the preface and introduction to this volume. The other eight can be viewed while reading the case study chapters.

¡VIVA! Community Arts and Popular Education in the Americas (23 minutes)

Produced by Maggie Hutcheson and Pato Esquivel

The VIVA! project is introduced, with its collaborators offering glimpses of the community arts projects in five countries, as well as international exchanges in Toronto, Panama, and Mexico, focusing on decolonizing art and education.

Kuna Children's Art Workshops (Panama) (15 minutes)

Produced by Laura Reinsborough

Between 1993 and 2000, Kuna communities off the coast of Panama involved children in a diverse range of cultural activities, using painting, theatre, dance, music, song, and poetry to recover cultural values and promote ecological consciousness.

The Personal Legacy Project (Canada) (12 minutes)

Produced by Heather Hermant

The Personal Legacy project developed by theatre artist Diane Roberts draws from West/Central African dance and story traditions to involve artists in probing their ancestral memories in a physical/dramaturgical process where the teller/dancer and the story/event are in a dynamic and changing relationship.

Jumblies Theatre (Canada) (12 minutes)

Produced by Maggie Hutcheson

Informed by the British community play movement, the Bridge of One Hair project of Jumblies Theatre has engaged many artists and residents in a culturally diverse west-end Toronto neighborhood in exploring diverse histories, identities, and bridges across their differences.

Telling Our Stories (Canada) (16 minutes)

Produced by Loreto Bravo and Lisa Campbell

In 2005–2006, the Catalyst Centre in Toronto brought together artist educators for a popular education train-the-trainer process that led them to design and facilitate projects with youth to explore and express their stories in many different artistic forms.

Cultural Marketplace / Tianguis Cultural (Mexico) (18 minutes)

Produced by Pato Esquivel

Organized in 1995 by activist youth in Guadalajara, Mexico, Tianguis Cultural weekly draws over two hundred

Maggie Hutcheson (Canada) and Pato Esquivel (Mexico), coproducers of VIVA! videos.

exhibitors (countercultural youth, Indigenous and solidarity groups, NGOs, artists of all kinds) and six thousand visitors to a cultural marketplace that offers a safe space for alternative urban identities and a noncommercial forum for interaction among groups that share a progressive social vision.

Painting by Listening (Mexico) (18 minutes)

Produced by Loreto Bravo and Heather Hermant

Through a training program for young artists/animators, Checo Valdez is developing and extending a unique process of engaging communities in community mural production that comes from the people themselves, and has been applied in communities from the Zapatista autonomous communities to Munich, Germany.

UCLA ArtsBridge (USA) (16 minutes)

Produced by Lisa Campbell-Salazar

UCLA ArtsBridge involves students in arts education residencies with inner-city schools in Los Angeles, nurturing the creativity of the diverse student bodies, cultivating mutually beneficial, respectful, and responsive relationships between the schools, community arts centers, and UCLArts.

BilwiVision Community TV (Nicaragua) (12 minutes)

Produced by BilwiVision staff directed by Reyna Armida Duarte

BilwiVision, the community television station of URACCAN, is developing an alternative practice of communications to reflect the cultural diversity of the Caribbean Coast of Nicaragua through their voices and images.

Index